WORTH
THE STRUGGLE

Dr. Althea L. Phillips

CLAY BRIDGES
PRESS

Worth the Struggle

ISBN: 978-1-939815-79-8
eISBN: 978-1-939815-99-6

DEDICATION

This book is dedicated to everyone who knows that the daily struggle with adversities is real but understands that through it all, the struggle is worth it in the end. For many people, learning to rejoice and be glad in the day that the Lord has made could be a struggle, especially when they are striving to live life with purpose while facing adversities and trying to embrace the lessons learned along the way.

This book is also dedicated to Jerry Lee Patrick, my ex-husband, friend, and father and stepfather to my adult children. Caring for him through his journey with amyotrophic lateral sclerosis (ALS) helped me to understand that the struggle to live life with purpose is worth it.

TABLE OF CONTENTS

INTRODUCTION

*This is the day that the L*ORD *has made; let us rejoice and be glad in it.*
—Ps. 118:24 ESV

"The day the LORD has made" is not limited to a 24-hour period lived in a day. The day the Lord has made is a process wrapped with all the things that can happen in pursuit of living life with purpose while learning to rejoice and be glad. The journey of pursuing a life lived with purpose often looks and feels like a struggle. However, it is this process that encompasses the core of who God is. The process of accepting that this is the day that the Lord has made empowers individuals to trust God. The struggle and all the things that it encompasses in pursuit of purpose look like wrapping paper. The wrapping paper used to cover the gifts given by God empowers individuals to uncover that they are really made in the likeness and image of God, especially when faced with adversity. Furthermore, it is learning how to be glad and rejoice while going through the process that fosters the realization that the struggle is worth it!

Worth the Struggle helps people understand how obstacles, challenges, adversities, and the adversary work like wrapping paper and are often used to cover up their destiny. Nevertheless, it is through this process that people will come to know who God is in the struggle. The process of knowing who God is facilitates the birthing of purpose in the lives of followers. True worshippers often will seek God's strategy in his plans for their lives rather than waiting to hear a yes or no to his will. God's strategy in "the day that the LORD has made," is more than a yes or no; it is a process that's implemented by faith. God used Jerry's illnesses—amyotrophic lateral sclerosis (ALS), depression, periods of suicidal ideations—and the dying process as a type of wrapping paper. The wrapping paper helped me to discover what God had put inside me for his glory. The wrapping paper was used to help uncover my purpose and hidden gifts as part of the process of living my life with purpose. I learned many lessons during the struggle, one of which was the removal of the wrapping paper created to temporarily house my destiny. Jesus said, "These things I have spoken unto you, that in me ye might have peace. In the world ye shall have tribulation: but be of good cheer; I have overcome the world" (John 16:33 KJV). Through Jerry's illness, I discovered that struggles are often sent as part of the process of finding purpose. This experience brought us closer together as parents and friends for God's glory. Looking back, I learned it was worth the struggle to live my life with purpose and that to live it meant that I had to seek first the kingdom of God and its righteousness. "For I know the thoughts that I think toward you, says the LORD, thoughts of peace and not of evil, to give you a future and a hope" (Jeremiah 29:11).

Worth the Struggle can be used to understand better how faith can be more effective in the day that the Lord has made, especially when the anointing and the appointed time appear to be at opposite ends. The space or gap between the anointing time and the appointed time could feel like a struggle for the anointed as they are stepping toward their appointed time. The anointing, calling, or purpose is a gift from God that is scheduled to be used at an appointed time for it to function effectively. Every person has a purpose given to make a unique difference in the lives of others. My purpose in this project is to help others see a deeper appreciation for discovering their purpose by the way of process and realizing that the struggle is worth it. How does one rejoice and be glad in the day that the Lord has made while in a struggle?

Taking care of my ex-husband Jerry during his illness with ALS was a trying journey for the family as well as for him. It brought me closer to understanding how to be glad and rejoice through the means of rest while in the midst of a struggle. In addition, it helped me understand the importance of living life with purpose. One way to cope effectively with the struggle is by discovering who God is through faith while working through the process. It is in this process that the problems and the promises of God appear to be dancing together with faith and fear and where bitter moments and blessings collaborate to help individuals in reaching their destiny.

You may experience being anointed while feeling that the appointed time is nowhere in view and subsequently realize that purpose and pain ride together side by side as companions. All of this is a part of the ordered steps in the day that the Lord has made. Learning how faith works helps people rejoice and be glad even when all the things that come with daily life activities appear to be a struggle—especially when they are faced with challenges while striving to live life with purpose. It is in the day the Lord has made that challenges, problems, adversities, and the adversary are used for people to see God as far greater than the struggle with which they are being confronted.

In *Worth the Struggle*, readers will become more aware of seeing their life journey as a process in preparation for purpose. They will become empowered by faith believing it is through process that their purpose is revealed—often by the way of struggle. Moreover, the reader will learn that the process works as a facilitator in bringing their anointing closer to the appointed time. It is not unusual for people to experience unforeseen challenges in the day that the Lord has made. It is our trusting and believing in who God is in the process that lets us rejoice and be glad knowing the struggle is worth it.

WRAPPING PAPER FOR
THE STRUGGLE

CHAPTER 1

*But the God of all grace, who hath called us unto his eternal
glory by Christ Jesus, after that ye have suffered a while, make
you perfect, stablish, strengthen, settle you.*

—1 Pet. 5:10 KJV

Many of the steps ordered by God in the process are covered with a type of wrapping paper made from life lessons to help develop individuals for purpose. Jesus became a type of wrapping paper to secure a gift that would provide people a personal relationship with God, not religion. The purpose of the wrapping paper for the struggle is, first, to draw people closer to knowing who God is and, second, to help them discover and live out their purpose. The wrapping paper used in the struggle helps individuals live life with purpose as they ultimately give up what they thought they had control over. Moreover, along the way, they learn to trust God, who controls everything including the process required to "perfect, stablish, strengthen, settle" them. "Then He said to them, 'Follow Me, and I will make you fishers of men.' They immediately left their nets and followed Him" (Matthew 4:19–20).

Traditionally, wrapping paper is used as a protective barrier to cover a gift and prevent others from seeing what the item is until the time has come for the gift's function or purpose to be revealed. Wrapping paper can also function as a precaution to protect the gift from being damaged due to poor handling. There are different types of wrapping paper for certain packages. Some packaging tends to be more challenging to remove than others when it is time to open or reveal the gift. The gift determines the type of wrapping material used; often the more valuable the gift, the more secure the type of wrapping material used; this sometimes makes it a struggle to expose the gift. I have experienced this in receiving several different types of wrapped gifts in the mail. Sometimes, I had to use kitchen tools such as a sharp knife or a pair of kitchen scissors, which are normally used in food preparation where the joints of meat or fish need to be separated.

Everyone likes receiving gifts or packages; however, removing the wrapping can be a difficult but necessary process to reveal what is inside. The wrapping paper used for this process with its challenges pushes me to the next level of understanding the importance of pursuing my purpose. At times, I had to overcome the struggle of removing the wrapping paper that God sent to see the hidden gift inside of me. Although challenging at times, the wrapping paper used in the struggle is never intended to discourage people from revealing their hidden gift.

Caring for Jerry during the process of ALS was one of the many wrapping papers I had to remove to progress toward the next level of discovering my purpose and who I am in "I Am" (one of the names of God that best describes to others who he is to them). Understanding why wrapping paper is used in the struggle to discover one's purpose begins now. "But we have this treasure in earthen vessels, that the excellence of the power may be of God and not of us" (2 Corinthians 4:7). Just before his recent death a few months ago, my ex-husband required hospice in addition to total care. While I was putting this project together, he was given a life expectancy of 18 months. He lived with this disease an additional 12 months. Our children and his sister-in-law helped me care for him, which required 24/7 attention. We became his hands, arms, and legs. Although he was able to ambulate, he was at high risk for falls because of the disease and loss of muscle tone. I have learned to worship God in the process while living with challenges. By God teaching me through challenges, I learned to live above adversities because I know that being glad and rejoicing in moments such as those pleases God. "Your sandals shall be iron and bronze; as your days, so shall your strength be" (Deuteronomy 33:25).

In doing so, I learned to trust God in every stage of the process. I used worship as a tool to help remove the wrapping paper that we faced as a family in caring for Jerry. For me, worship was an expression of the fineness of the power that came from God, not of me. Needless to say, it was God's strength I found in my core that gave me the support I needed for each day to be Jerry's hands, legs, and feet.

Becoming a bondservant to Christ afforded me the chance to minister to Jerry as he went through the bereavement process. Living as a believer amid the daily struggles prepared me for this project. God gave me revelations from adversities within the struggle as a light in seeking the kingdom of God and its righteousness. In the process, I learned the value of rejoicing and being glad in the day the Lord has made, regardless of adversities. The truth is that God has instructed every person to rejoice and be glad, which makes the struggle worth going through because he has already given them the end before the beginning. God is omniscient. Because he is all-knowing, he has the power to reassure people that they will get the victory in every circumstance before the end of time. God has promised that the purpose he has placed beneath the wrapped paper will be revealed regardless of the struggles faced as the wrapping paper is removed in the process. Although removing the wrapping in the process of discovering who God is and what the believer's purpose is may appear challenging, he has given his word that it will come to pass. "Declaring the end from the beginning, and from ancient times things that are not yet done" (Isaiah 46:10). God has given a day that he has made, but he is instructing believers to declare the end before the beginning. This is best accomplished by faith in knowing who God is while rejoicing and being glad in it.

Rejoicing and being glad is a form of worship in support of coping more effectively with adversities, struggles, or challenges. Being glad and rejoicing in the day the Lord has made is not limited to an emotional reaction but is a response to who the Lord is by his grace and through revelation. "And He said to me, 'My grace is sufficient for you, for My strength is made perfect in weakness'" (2 Corinthians 12:9). My prayer is for the grace of God to help people understand the role of the wrapping paper, so that we may understand who Jesus is in the process of discovering our destiny:

> Who shall bring a charge against God's elect? It is God who justifies. Who is he who condemns? It is Christ who died, and furthermore is also risen, who is even at the right hand of God, who also makes intercession for us. Who shall separate us from the love of Christ? Shall tribulation, or distress, or persecution, or famine, or nakedness, or peril, or sword? As it is written: "For Your sake we are killed all day long; We are accounted as sheep for the slaughter." Yet in all these things we are more than conquerors through Him who loved us. For I am persuaded that neither death nor life, nor angels nor principalities nor powers, nor things present nor things to come, nor height nor depth, nor any other created thing, shall be able to separate us from the love of God which is in Christ Jesus our LORD.
>
> —Rom. 8:33–39

When we acknowledge who Jesus is in our struggles, everything and everyone who stands against the purpose placed in them must submit to who Jesus is. The process often starts by removing the wrapping paper used to cover up our purpose. We can be glad in the day the Lord has made in spite of life encounters that appear to be giants in our eyes and in the eyes of others. Through seeking the kingdom of God first, followers will discover the mindset of Jesus along the journey. Having the mindset of Jesus empowers individuals to think like God during struggles while being led to victory by the Holy Spirit. The mindset of Jesus Christ is a thought process that allows the mind to perceive things the way God sees people, places, and things, not according to our normal thought process. The experiences learned from having the same thought process as Jesus will empower individuals to realize that his mindset governs their steps. These steps move followers toward their destiny even when adversity arises. Can one rejoice and be glad in the midst of struggles and see that struggle is worth it? The answer lies in getting to know who you are or your purpose in "I Am."

Adversities or struggles can be perceived as wrapping paper that covers the day the Lord has made. The wrapping paper is not meant to discourage believers from discovering the gift God has given them. It distracts others from seeing your gift before you are ready to operate and function in the gift. Believers may become easily sidetracked by the wrapping paper, affecting their ability to rejoice and be glad in the day the Lord has made. God's gift to Noah, who never saw rain, was to build an ark. However, God used rain as wrapping paper to cover the gift of Noah giving the world another chance to know God by developing a personal relationship with him:

> *The earth also was corrupt before God, and the earth was filled with violence. So God looked upon the earth, and indeed it was corrupt; for all flesh had corrupted their way on the earth. And God said to Noah, "The end of all flesh has come before Me, for the earth is filled with violence through them; and behold, I will destroy them with the earth. Make yourself an ark of gopherwood; make rooms in the ark, and cover it inside and outside with pitch."*
>
> —Gen. 6:11–14

In Noah's case, the wrapping paper was something he had never seen or experienced before in his lifetime. The wrapping paper God chose had to be massive in its destruction, where rainwater worked as a tool in preparation for his son, Jesus, to be a gift to the world. "A man's gift maketh room for him, and bringeth him before great men"

(Proverbs 18:16 KJV). God has a strategy for gifts to be placed inside his creations, often wrapping them with what appear to be adversities, hardship, destruction, illness, and even death. These hidden gifts are the answers to unresolved problems for mankind. The challenge for some believers is learning to overlook the struggle and remove the wrapping paper that hides the gift within.

I have a young adult child who willfully hangs out with a group of people to smoke marijuana and other controlled substances. I hate even the thought that this child, or any one of my eight children, is putting themselves at risk for danger. There was a time when I would allow myself to become angry about the situation. One day, I realized why I allowed myself to become angry about his choice to smoke marijuana and take other controlled substances. From the day he was born, every time I saw him headed toward danger, I would physically grab him and pull him out of a situation that appeared harmful to him. Now that he is an adult, my counsel against smoking marijuana or other controlled substances has become ineffective. In this case, what worked years ago in protecting him doesn't work now. This thought worried me until God reminded me that he is omniscient and omnipresent. So, instead of worrying about something that I once had influence and control over, I now worship. The wrapping paper used in my experience with my son was for me to come to a point of letting go and letting God by worshipping and not worrying. In the process of living life with purpose, there are life lessons that God will use to motivate people to worship him. In this struggle, I learned that I could no longer physically and verbally protect my child, and as a result I had to acknowledge and trust a God who is omnipresent and omniscient in the situation. The experience prompted me to remove myself as a type of wrapping paper in order for the gift to be exposed—the gift is God in me. God will often select situations where people have lost control in the areas they once controlled just so they can be reminded who he is.

When believers understand that they are losing control over things they once had control over, it helps to further their progress in becoming glad and rejoicing in the day the Lord has made. Trusting God as the one who is omnipresent and omniscient in spite of the challenges it takes to remove the wrapping paper is a game changer, but the struggle is worth it. At times in the eyes of followers, the wrapping paper around the gift God has given them may seem like a giant, leaving them feeling overwhelmed because of the struggle. However, the challenge of working with and through struggles is never bigger than the purpose God placed inside a believer. Trust in God and not the giants that show up in the form of wrapping paper. Rejoicing and being glad in the day is accomplished through worship and trusting the one who created the day. This is the day the Lord has made; it was created so that all people, including nonbelievers, would see God for who he is over any problem, challenge, or adversity. Focus not on the challenge or struggles but on the one who has the power to resurrect and give life to the dry bones of our struggles. Challenges with struggles prompt followers to see faith as a required substance essential to rejoicing and being glad in the day the Lord has made. God is the answer to every problem and the solution to every challenge. Trust and worship him. Our attempts to resolve problems may not always be God's solution. Trusting him takes the place of our self-righteousness.

Worshippers see God in the day he has made as an opportunity to look to him as the author and finisher of their faith regardless of any unseen adversity or adversary.

Thus says the LORD: "Cursed is the man who trusts in man and makes flesh his strength, whose heart departs from the LORD. For he shall be like a shrub in the desert, and shall not see when good comes, but shall inhabit the parched places in the wilderness, in a salt land which is not inhabited. Blessed is the man who trusts in the LORD, and whose hope is the LORD. For he shall be like a tree planted by the waters, which spreads out its roots by the river, and will not fear when heat comes."

—Jer. 17:5–8

While discovering their purpose, true worshippers acknowledge God's faithfulness before the manifestation. He is committed to every purpose placed inside his creation, and he has promised that it will do what he purposes it to do. Knowing who God is empowers true worshippers to be glad and joyful throughout the process because they know what to expect. Their expectation comes from having the same mindset that is in Jesus, which gives access to his presence and to the kingdom of God. True worshippers join him at the table already anticipating that their thirst and hunger will be satisfied with more than enough. Being in the presence of God is like feasting at an all-you-can-eat buffet. I love to visit an all-you-can-eat buffet restaurant. I anticipate what I will eat before arriving. I appreciate the assortment of food to choose from. Before entering, like a true worshipper, I already have in mind a song of praise with thanksgiving. Once there, I just need to take the time to find or discover my desired food items, knowing that this is a part of the process of dining. As followers, you enter in his presence with praise and thanksgiving because everything related to your purpose is in "I Am." Finding what you are looking for at the feast is similar to finding "I Am"; the thing you are looking for is in the process he has prepared for you. This expression of a person's purpose is not what they do for a living but who they are. We are created in God's image and likeness; it is his spirit that empowers people to say, "I am with purpose," like God does in describing who we are. The great "I Am" has given everyone a purpose; this gift empowers believers to say "I am." The I am or purpose in people works as a gift to produce the likeness of who God is at his core. "For with God nothing will be impossible" (Luke 1:37).

"For the eyes of the Lord run to and fro throughout the whole earth, to show Himself strong on behalf of those whose heart is loyal to Him" (2 Chronicles 16:9). God looks for true worshippers throughout the earth who can embrace process. Individuals with this type of heart can acknowledge God for who he is. Furthermore, they are willing to go through the process before reaching their appointed time in fulfilling their purpose. What brings true worshippers into being? It's the level of trust and belief they have in the one who stands behind the promises he made to people who believe. When God speaks a word, he is faithful to his word. Faith is the substance of seeing the promises of his word come to fruition, which includes the plans, destinies, and purposes he has for all his creations. The key to a believer's journey and the steps that lead to one's destiny in God come from understanding what faith is. For believers who delight themselves in God, he will grant them the desires of their hearts. The true desires of believers' hearts are not based on an emotional reaction from having a great day but based on knowing that the greatest part of any day is believing that God is in control and that he has the best interest of everyone in his heart. "Be anxious for nothing, but in everything by prayer and supplication, with thanksgiving, let your requests be made known to God; and the peace of God, which surpasses all understanding, will guard your hearts and minds through Christ Jesus" (Philippians 4:6–7).

The desire in the hearts of followers is to seek what God has for them, believing it is the best plan concerning their purpose even if most of the work is developed in what appears to be the dark. Good soil for plants often appears dark, yet it is rich with minerals that promote growth. Sometimes, unexpected steps toward process can be viewed as dark moments, struggles, and challenging times for followers, especially when God selects them to use as a tool to unwrap their purpose. In the process, I had to learn that the true power source behind my purpose was the Holy Spirit, who comforts me during the struggle and unexpected steps in dark times. God's thoughtful strategy ensures me that he is in control from the day of anointing to the appointed time. Moreover, from the unwrapping to the day of revealing, the things learned in the struggle make going through the process worth it.

Until I wrote this book, I never really understood that even though God, my heavenly father is in control of everything all the time, I still found myself despising the struggle sometimes. It was in these moments when I learned that faith had to become my new way of thinking, especially when I found myself feeling one way, but God was telling me to do something totally opposite of what I was feeling. In doing so, I had to learn to change my old way of seeing things to a mindset that needed to be kept on Jesus's thought process. Believers are taught from Hebrews 11:1 that "faith is the substance of things hoped for, the evidence of things not seen." God's word taught me that I needed to believe Jesus's mindset is the substance of things to hope for. My hope in writing this book was believing that Jesus would direct me in writing a message to help others in the struggle by hearing his word and by his spirit. Moreover, the work at that time was not yet completed; the promise I had from Jesus as the author and finisher of my faith became my foundation, knowing that what he had started, he would finish. I learned by faith in spite of my imperfections that Jesus is the best author and way-maker for me to live life with purpose even though I am still a work in progress. Dark moments in the process can be a struggle for followers when questions and doubts become most prevalent.

However, everything we ask for in Jesus's name during the process will be given because he is the storyteller and the ink source that allows the pen in us to write the new narrative pertaining to purpose:

> *Therefore do not worry, saying, "What shall we eat?" or "What shall we drink?" or "What shall we wear?" For after all these things the Gentiles seek. For your heavenly Father knows that you need all these things. But seek first the kingdom of God and His righteousness, and all these things shall be added to you.*
>
> —Matt. 6:31–33

God instructs followers to seek first the kingdom of God and its righteousness, and all these things will be added to them. When believers know the thoughts of God, their destiny is revealed: "In all your ways acknowledge Him, and He shall direct your paths" (Proverbs 3:6). People who search for their true identity before discovering who God is put the cart in front of the horse. Seeking the kingdom of God first before all things that he has made provides people an opportunity to know him as the one who made all things possible. Purposely seeking God as the one who made all things first is a form of worship, and like a key, worship opens the door to wisdom.

In Psalm 37:4, God instructs his believers to "delight thyself also in the LORD: and he shall give thee the desires of thine heart" (KJV). Everything that God has placed in you concerning your true identity and purpose is revealed or discovered in the process of seeking the kingdom of God daily and believing that he is who he said he is. In this search, rejoicing and being glad becomes the platform for God's promises as a provider and one who is faithful to his word. Seeking the by-products or the fruit of the seed first will have a negative influence in your understanding of how the kingdom of God functions. It is this mindset that perceives resources such as income, employment, food, clothing, land, relationships with others, and shelter as being our first priority rather than knowing who God is being our first priority. This mindset doesn't seek first the one who created the fruit of the seed or the by-products. Needless to say, it is this same thought process of seeking these things first that places people at risk for viewing things as a type of god. Seeking first the kingdom of God is the way to live life with purpose—by knowing the creator first.

The process of seeking the kingdom of God creates a personal relationship with him through Jesus. The process of seeking the kingdom of God becomes much clearer in the struggle when the old way of thinking is unwrapped, exposing the mindset of Jesus. As individuals learn to live life with purpose, they will discover Jesus never intended to be a guild in the process; rather, he is to be perceived as the process: "Jesus said to him, 'I am the way, the truth, and the life. No one comes to the Father except through Me'" (John 14:6). The old way of thinking is the mindset prior to letting the same mind that's in Christ Jesus become our new normal way of thinking.

In 2012, I returned to school to get a master's degree in nursing. During the first week of class, we were given a written assignment. After I submitted the assignment, my professor instructed me to do it over and this time, "Write as a scholar." I called her and asked her what she meant by saying that I was "to write my assignment as a scholar." I reminded her that I just graduated with my bachelor's degree in nursing a couple of months before and that this was my first written assignment in a master's program. The struggle for me was I could not adapt from my old way of thinking to her way of thinking. I felt it was unfair for her to want me to meet her expectation of thinking in the first week of class. After speaking with her, I learned that her expectation of me was not going to change. Needless to say, I had to change the way I saw myself by changing the way I think. She saw me as a scholar although my written work did not reflect it at first. Soon after, my written work was of a scholarly voice, but my writing didn't start to change until I realized that my old mindset had to be transformed first. I had everything I needed to get a master's degree in nursing; however, I had to change the way I thought about myself as a scholar in spite of my struggles of coping with a learning disability. I had to first believe that I could do it by changing the way I thought about myself, and I found the support I needed to improve my writing skills to match what was expected of me as a student. I had what it took to complete the program; however, I needed help from others to pull out what I had inside me so that I could write as a scholar.

People, like seeds, are equipped by God to be fruitful, and because they are created in his likeness and image, they are destined to create and be creative in spite of struggles. It is God's doing when the fruit of the seed produces a wealthy return of things that are often sought after. However, in the process of understanding the kingdom of God and its righteousness, it is by the way of a changed mindset and by his spirit that people are empowered to seek the kingdom first, not things. Jesus said, "I am the vine, you are the branches. He who abides in Me, and I in him, bears much fruit; for without Me you can do nothing" (John 15:5).

The apple tree doesn't seek after the apples it produces. Apples are produced when an apple seed is planted. Similar to seeds that are planted to produce fruit, purpose is also planted in people to produce what they were created to do; however, God has designed it to come by the way of process. There is a challenging struggle in the process, and that is having to work from the ground up. Seeking first the kingdom of God is an invitation from him for people to see themselves as being gifted with seeds of greatness but having to work from ground zero. The invitation is the starting place from ground zero up. It is given in hope that people will discover and live their purpose by knowing God through Jesus as the one who is the way for them to succeed. The focus should not be placed on discovery but on living the purpose God has for you. Society as we know it, prepares people to look for work to function effectively in their community. Because purpose is planted from within, individuals don't need to look for it, but they need to unwrap the paper by beginning the process of knowing who created them to do what they were purposed to do. Ground zero is believing that God has already equipped us with everything we need to be effective in our purpose. God created each seed that he plants to be righteously ripe for purpose, and it is not the seed's own doing that causes it to be fruitful, but his righteousness. "For your heavenly Father knows that you need all these things" (Matthew 6:32).

Rejoicing and being glad when faced with difficulties can be challenging for anyone, especially when a seed is coming from the ground up; however, it is worth the struggle. "For who has despised the day of small things? For these . . . rejoice." (Zechariah 4:10). Faith as it relates to seeing your purpose in the beginning phase often looks undeveloped. Faith becomes most effective when individuals have a mindset like Jesus:

> *Let this mind be in you, which was also in Christ Jesus: Who, being in the form of God, thought it not robbery to be equal with God: But made himself of no reputation, and took upon him the form of a servant, and was made in the likeness of men.*
> —Phil. 2:5–7 KJV

Recently, I was speaking to a friend about how frustrating the time between the anointing and my appointed time is for me. I expressed my feelings of frustration by reflecting on the gap between David's anointing and his appointed time and the experiences he went through in the meantime:

> *Thus Jesse made seven of his sons pass before Samuel. And Samuel said to Jesse, "The LORD has not chosen these." And Samuel said to Jesse, "Are all the young men here?" Then he*

said, "There remains yet the youngest, and there he is, keeping the sheep." And Samuel said to Jesse, "Send and bring him. For we will not sit down till he comes here." So he sent and brought him in. Now he was ruddy, with bright eyes, and good-looking. And the LORD said, "Arise, anoint him; for this is the one!" Then Samuel took the horn of oil and anointed him in the midst of his brothers; and the Spirit of the LORD came upon David from that day forward.

—1 Sam. 16:10–13

There have been times during the process that I felt a little annoyed about many of the things I went through in living life with purpose. Moreover, I had to learn not to despise starting out in small beginnings. I would sometimes wonder whether all the challenges were necessary and whether the struggle was really worth it. I reflected on my experience working as a staff nurse on a locked psychiatric unit and compared it with David attending sheep when he was anointed as king over Israel but then returned to keeping sheep. Daily, I would get dressed in the role of a staff nurse, desperately eager for what I was created to do but feeling frustrated in the process of reaching my appointed time. Faith taught me that in spite of the small beginnings as a staff nurse, God had already imparted my destiny to me, but in the meantime, my job was a type of workout room designed to prepare me for the next level in reaching my destiny. In the time between operating in purpose and the appointed time, I was chosen to perform a specific task. Soon after, I began to appreciate the benefits of small beginnings in the process of pursuing life on purpose.

It was in the small beginnings that I learned on a smaller scale what I was chosen to do. I recall that in the fourth grade, I was failing all of the major subjects. My teacher and my mother met to discuss an alternative educational plan. My teacher at that time could not see how I could pass the fourth grade unless something changed to improve my chances of learning more effectively. When we arrived home, I asked my mother what my teacher had said, and my mother told me that my teacher did not see me as a behavioral problem in the classroom, but she said that I spent half the day asking other students how their day was. When I finally sat down to do classwork, school was half over. To this day, I still find myself drawn to the concerns of my peers and what they are going through versus becoming astute in what society has prescribed for learners to know in a classroom setting.

"Despise not the days of small beginnings" is a motto for followers who have learned an appreciation of purpose even though it appears to be without form. Some may feel frustrated in the days of small beginnings. I can see more clearly that my small beginnings may have started in a fourth-grade classroom where I found myself drawn to care for the heart and concerns of my peers.

Rejoicing and being glad can be difficult when others don't validate your purpose. Distraction allows followers to focus more on despising the lessons learned than fostering a mindset of helping individuals prepare for their purpose. This mindset is required to rejoice and be glad in who God is, not what he has done or is about to do. Believers are faithful to the one who created the day and not the stuff that takes place throughout the day.

"Though He slay me, yet will I trust Him" (Job 13:15). To help better understand how worshippers come to celebrate each day the Lord has made, take a look at typical sports fans. The responses and reactions toward their favorite team before and after the game come from great faithfulness. Fans' love, commitment, and zealousness toward their teams are not based on a team's successes or losses during the season or what they did or did not do in the past several seasons. The core of fans' commitment to their teams stems from a personal connection they have with their teams. Sports fans exercise a type of worship toward a team even though most have never met the players in person. So why does it appear so abstract for some believers to worship the God who loved the world by sending his only son, Jesus, as a mediator between man and God? Yet some followers show a minimal level of excitement toward Jesus, who saved lives, changed their lives forever, and promised life more abundantly to believers.

Sports fans raise their voices in excitement before leaving the house and before reaching the field—all this and more before the game starts. "Now faith is the substance of things hoped for, the evidence of things not seen" (Hebrews 11:1). "When Jesus came into the region of Caesarea Philippi, He asked His disciples, saying, 'Who do men say that I, the Son of Man, am?'" (Matthew 16:13). The substance of faith makes it powerful when activated. Similarly, knowing who Jesus is and not just the position he has makes our faith in Jesus powerful when activated.

God wants believers to face everything that the day may bring with faith. Believers who choose to worship in spirit and in truth are aligned with God. Their thoughts of rejoicing and being glad become their priority, rather than focusing on adversities or challenges. Sports fans might have a better concept of how to worship. Their excitement, commitment, and love for their team is imbued by their rejoicing and being glad before the team enters the field. Imagine people visualizing God as their favorite sports team and seeing the day the Lord has made as the game. Believers who embrace this concept will understand better the importance of worship before struggling with any challenge or adversity. Committed sports fans are devoted to their teams in the same way that true worshippers are committed to acknowledging who God is in spite of what type of day they are having. True worshippers, like devoted sports fans, are faithful in rejoicing and being glad before, after, and during the contest. True worshippers' commitment does not rest on winning but on who God is as their source for winning. God is teaching people that having joy and being glad does not come from the things that they can see now, but it will come by faith in the things that they hope for. Such confidence comes from knowing the one who made the day. True worshippers do not wait until victory is evident to believe in God. On the contrary, true worshippers through faith acknowledge the truth about who God is without the need of natural evidence to support their joy. I believe God used Jerry's illness and dying process to bring out the living word of Jesus that's inside me to touch the lives of others. God used me to minister to Jerry by becoming the hands, arms, and feet of Jesus. This became truly an awesome experience for me to see Jesus work as the resurrection and the life in our lives.

Two years ago, Jerry and I hardly spoke to each other. At that time, we elected to feed bitterness by not seeing the better in each other as imperfect people. In 2017, I bought a house and created a living space out of my family room; I moved Jerry in and became his primary caregiver. I believed the day would come when Jerry would say,

> I didn't die alone because when I was hungry Jesus used you to feed me. When I needed to be changed, you clothed me. When I needed help to go to the bathroom, you took me and cleaned up after me. When I cursed God and wanted to commit suicide, you listened and comforted me by not judging me. You provided transportation and escorted me to my doctors' appointments. Jesus, you even made sure that my children were around me during the painful and most challenging time of my life, and for that, God, you get the glory.

I knew that Jerry would most likely pass away as the doctors predicted. However, nobody would be able to say, "Jesus, if only you were here, his life would have been so much better." God used me and our children as a type of Jesus for Jerry in the disease process. Moreover, in the role as his primary caregiver and friend, I can say the struggle was worth it. God allowed me to see the relationship between Jerry and me resurrected from the grave after the divorce and transformed into an abundant life in spite of having to live with ALS.

God expects his creations to rejoice and to be glad daily in spite of facing bad situations. To worship is to rejoice and to be glad in the God who created the day. Worship should not be founded solely on emotions but on knowing the truth of who God is. God is looking for people who are willing to seek and trust in who he is through faith. He uses our dysfunctions or difficult circumstances as opportunities to bring out the callings and gifts he placed deep within us so that we can function effectively in their purpose. Consequently, followers will be able to be glad and rejoice not by what they see today but by faith and trust in the one who created the day along with the dysfunctions and difficult circumstances. In every outcome, being glad from a believer's standpoint is to understand who God is. This mindset trusts that God will provide believers with perfect peace because their thoughts are transformed to be like his thoughts: "Thou wilt keep him in perfect peace, whose mind is stayed on thee: because he trusteth in thee" (Isaiah 26:3 KJV).

Coping with dyslexia brings me some unique pressing struggles. God never healed me from my disability. However, he taught me that his grace and mercy are far greater than my disability. And it took years, but he answered one of the biggest questions for someone with a learning disability: Why me? At times, unanswered questions can be pressing and challenging. However, an internal power such as God's grace moves some followers to press even harder than the adversary or the adversity they are struggling with.

Having a mind that has been transformed to think like Jesus facilitates a person's purpose as a gift that glorifies God because it is based on how he thinks and his will. "And be not conformed to this world: but be ye transformed by the renewing of your mind, that ye may prove what is that good, and acceptable, and perfect, will of God" (Romans 12:2 KJV). Being Jesus-like-minded empowers individuals to trust God over anything that happens in any given situation, good or bad, throughout the day while realizing he is greater than anything and in any given situation. Believers walk by faith, not by sight. It is with the natural eye that people often see difficult circumstances as complicated situations. This often causes people to react rather than to respond because they have not gotten in touch with the greater one who lives inside them. Consequently, when people see faith as their source of strength from within, it empowers them to respond differently from what is perceived by their natural eyes. Several times in my walk with God, like Peter, I found myself walking on water until an unexpected wind came. In these moments, I found myself falling and yelling for God to help me. I felt disappointed and discouraged in myself because I felt that I had failed by not keeping my focus on God. In hindsight, I understand that questioning my position in the process of transformation is also part of the journey of discovering the me that God sees as it relates to identity and purpose.

The transformation process is a period in which people change their mindset into what God has called, shaped, equipped, formed, and set aside for his glory. I remember periods of my transformation process when I felt frustrated in the thoughts that I had toward my job. I told God that perhaps it might be better if he would consider choosing someone else who would be a better fit for his plan.

At that time, I was going through a challenging shift at work as charge nurse and felt that God was taking too long in preparing me to operate fully in my purpose. Early one morning, God spoke to me with such mercy and with a loving voice. He said, "Althea, I want you to think about the process of a caterpillar and what it has to do to become a butterfly." God gently enlightened me that I was a butterfly inside of a cocoon but in an inchworm's body. He explained that I was in a transitional stage where I had been anointed but not yet appointed to the position he set aside for my purpose. He explained that my frustrations and discouragements with struggles were gifts and not a curse. These feelings are what people often perceive as weak spots. However, the pillars in the process can be used to support the discovery of one's purpose. God, on the other hand, will allow people to use these feelings of uncertainty to move them in tight spaces, to weaken the walls of the cocoon that will push them into the next level of their destiny. These hardships, often perceived as facts, turn our weakness into an opportunity for the Holy Spirit, who represents the truth to empower those who are being pressed for greatness. This explains why the cocoon stage is a gift and not a curse. It's a fact that caterpillars are a type of worm that uses the ground as its mode of transportation, whereas butterflies get around in the air. The truth is that the caterpillar's destiny is to be a butterfly, not the caterpillar it is today.

"Not by might nor by power, but by My Spirit, says the LORD of hosts" (Zechariah 4:6). God uses our cocoon to insulate us in our weakest hour when we are feeling most challenged by naysayers, haters, disappointments, or a lack of validation from others. "When they stood him among the pillars, Samson said to the servant who held his hand, 'Put me where I can feel the pillars that support the temple, so that I may lean against them'" (Judges 16:25–26 NIV). As followers, we need to look for pillars as doors during the process for support to bring us closer to our destiny. Facts can be viewed as supporting evidence that can work for you in a courtroom, for example, or work against you if another attorney can find a way to have them dismissed. Facts were never intended to take the place of the truth; although, facts are often used as an alternative for the truth. In some cases, facts got people locked up in jail, but it was the truth that set them free. In Samson's case, facts were gathered to have him locked up; then his eyes were gouged out, and he was chained to two pillars only to be humiliated by the Philistines. But it was the truth that he knew who God is in his personal walk and his faithfulness toward purpose that empowered Samson to pray and ask God for help in fulfilling his purpose.

Facts are often disguised as pillars for followers pursuing the truth of their purpose. Pillars viewed only as facts keep people from discovering their destiny. The pillars were like facts in the life of Samson used as wrapping paper to cover up the truth of what he was created to do. Often in the pursuit of destiny, truth and facts start out as enemies but become allies in the fight for justice and freedom. The same pillars were used to support the Philistines' attempt to destroy Samson, but God allowed him to see them as a support beam and destroy thousands of Philistines in one gathering.

Believers who have a personal and intimate relationship with God learn that all circumstances are subject to the truth of who God is. This concept helps believers understand that the power that lies in Jesus is the same as the one that controls the pen to their story. In other words, knowing what God says about a circumstance becomes the absolute truth. The truth, not facts, sets people free to have an abundant relation-

24

ship with God. Sticking purely to the facts places circumstances above God, whereas truth gives rise to who God is over every circumstance:

> *No weapon that is formed against thee shall prosper; and every tongue that shall rise against thee in judgment thou shalt condemn. This is the heritage of the servants of the LORD, and their righteousness is of me, saith the LORD.*
>
> —Isa. 54:17 KJV

What God has said concerning weapons stands to be the absolute truth. It is a fact that weapons will be formed against you because of your calling and purpose. But because of who God is, no weapon can destroy the purpose that God has placed inside you. As 1 Samuel 16 says, although David was anointed as king over Israel, he was not the people's choice, and after he was anointed, he had to return to keeping the sheep. Jesse had eight sons, and the youngest of them was David. He was not considered highly by his brothers or his father; in many cases, he was considered as an afterthought. At this time, Israel was going through a season in which God had rejected the king the people had selected:

> *Now the LORD said to Samuel, "How long will you mourn for Saul, seeing I have rejected him from reigning over Israel? Fill your horn with oil, and go; I am sending you to Jesse the Bethlehemite. For I have provided Myself a king among his sons."*
>
> —1 Sam. 16:1

God instructed the prophet Samuel that the next king of Israel would be one of Jesse's sons and that he would let Samuel know which one of the eight was to be king when the oil was poured from the horn for the anointing.

> *Thus Jesse made seven of his sons pass before Samuel. And Samuel said to Jesse, "The LORD has not chosen these." And Samuel said to Jesse, "Are all the young men here?" Then he*

said, "There remains yet the youngest, and there he is, keeping the sheep." And Samuel said to Jesse, "Send and bring him. For we will not sit down till he comes here." So he sent and brought him in. Now he was ruddy, with bright eyes, and good-looking. And the Lord said, "Arise, anoint him; for this is the one!" Then Samuel took the horn of oil and anointed him in the midst of his brothers; and the Spirit of the Lord came upon David from that day forward.

—1 Sam. 16:10–13

Although the facts appeared to outweigh David's purpose and calling, in due time, the truth overruled the facts. It was a fact that David was almost overlooked by his father and his brothers as the anointed one. At the time of David's anointing, he tended sheep. Preparing a king is similar to the process of a caterpillar transforming into a butterfly. The facts or one's past cannot define or describe the truth concerning one's destiny. It's a fact that caterpillars are a type of worm that uses the ground as its mode of transportation, whereas butterflies get around in the air. The truth is the caterpillar's destiny is to be a butterfly, not the caterpillar it is today. There is a saying that "the truth will set you free." God sees a person's purpose as truth. He doesn't dwell on the facts surrounding an individual's current circumstance or past actions. God uses the truth rather than facts to reveal who we truly are. He uses his love through truth to free people from the lack of knowledge and a mindset based on facts or the things we see. "And the Lord will make you the head and not the tail; you shall be above only, and not beneath" (Deuteronomy 28:13).

God imparts truth in the spirit of people so that they become empowered to overcome facts that are barriers to reaching purpose. "God is Spirit, and those who worship Him must worship in spirit and truth" (John 4:24). The Holy Spirit reveals to true worshippers who God is and how he sees them based on the truth. True worshippers become excited when the Holy Spirit reveals to them who God is and how he sees them in truth. Worship experiences force facts to submit to truth. Even the

US court system seeks truth over facts: "Do you solemnly swear/affirm that you will tell the truth, the whole truth, and nothing but the truth, so help you God?" In society, we walk by sight and by facts, but in the world of faith, we walk by truth. Truth separates true worshippers from all others. Faith supports and engulfs truth, leaving facts defenseless. Truth becomes the new normal for believers. Faith gravitates to areas where the impossible becomes the new normal of possibilities. Truth takes a much higher precedence over facts, and it's the concept that puts a believer's faith into action. It is the very essence of truth that supports the substance of faith and not facts. It's also a fact that people often find themselves waiting for God. But the truth of the matter is that God is waiting for people to find their purpose. "Open the gates, that the righteous nation which keeps the truth may enter in" (Isaiah 26:2).

Poor choices and the consequences that follow often come dressed with regret; however, as it relates to purpose-driven individuals' mistakes, the consequences cannot keep them from having purpose. Destiny should be perceived as something more powerful than past struggles; although, struggles also have their place. From struggles, people generally learn to appreciate success on the road to their destiny. Out of our struggle, success is born; from pain, we celebrate pleasure. Careers are developed from hard work, and higher education costs in time, money, and sacrifice. Understand that this is the day the Lord has made is a process to see the facts but also to learn diligently by faith to seek the truth. In this mindset, people can appreciate rejoicing and being glad in the struggle knowing the God who made the day is I Am. The struggles experienced in this process facilitate transformation, bringing change to fruition where "worth the struggle" is the new narrative of your story, which is no longer limited to facts.

"He made known to us the mystery of his will according to his good pleasure, which he purposed in Christ" (Ephesians 1:9 NIV). The journey to rejoicing and being glad is successfully done by understanding worship; although, for some, understanding true worship is a mystery. One can solve the mystery in understanding true worship by knowing who God is through Jesus Christ, which is his way and pleasure in understanding him. Jesus is the only way of knowing who God is; he is the source of our faith; for without faith, it is impossible to please God.

Revelation is God's method of unveiling things that must be learned to appreciate the steps he has ordered toward your purpose. Believers learn through faith that no matter what happens in the day the Lord has made, sooner or later it will work out for their good: "And we know that all things work together for good to them that love God, to them who are the called according to his purpose" (Romans 8:28 KJV). The Lord has a plan for us that decrees his purpose for people; the Bible refers to this in Jeremiah 29:11. His will is not a mystery for people who have a personal relationship with him and who believe that his plan for them to have purpose will succeed in spite of any circumstantial facts that can be used against what God has declare.

In Jeremiah 1:5, God shares with his believers that he not only knew them before he formed them, but he also set them apart for a journey to take them to their destiny. God sees, thinks, moves, and plans for his creations futuristically. When he sees people, he sees not where they have come from but where they are going. God sees each day that he makes as a journey that will take his creations to their destiny. Believers need to see the way God sees, which gives rise to him exposing believers to the end of their destiny before the beginning. God is omniscient and sees where all his creations are going before they reach their destiny. When believers rejoice and are glad in the day he has made, they're saying, in a form of worship, that God is faithful. "The eyes of your understanding being enlightened; that you may know what the hope of His calling, what are the riches of the glory of His inheritance in the saints" (Ephesians 1:18) The sight of a believer is faith. This sight guides believers to walk by faith and not by their natural eyesight. Faith becomes their new way of seeing. "Being confident of this very thing, that he which hath begun a good work in you will perform it until the day of Jesus Christ" (Philippians 1:6 KJV). Developing a follower's faith is often done through cultivating an intimate, personal relationship with God through Jesus, because the word he speaks gives life to people who listen and believe. "So then faith cometh by hearing, and hearing by the word of God" (Romans 10:17 KJV). Our spiritual ears that hear the word of God encourage faith to come in and take root. The way we process the word of God in our minds promotes a mindset like that of Jesus to be developed, where a believer's choices as well as behavior become more effective in purpose. "And do not be conformed to this world, but be transformed by the renewing of your mind, that you may prove what is that good and acceptable and perfect will of God" (Romans 12:2).

Faith came to Mary when she heard words spoken by God, the Holy Spirit, and her son, Jesus. She kept them hidden in her heart and was not distracted by her distressed circumstance. She believed in who Jesus is in her every circumstance. And when they ran out of wine, the mother of Jesus said to him in John 2:3–5: "'They have no wine.' Jesus said to her, 'Woman, what does your concern have to do with Me? My hour has not yet come.' His mother said to the servants, 'Whatever He says to you, do it.'" Jesus was waiting for Mary to reflect on the words that she kept hidden in her heart, to move her to see Jesus as the son of God. It wasn't until the day the wine ran out that Mary worked her faith to a whole new level. Mary used what she knew about Jesus as the author and finisher of her faith to address an unexpected wine deficit during a wedding celebration. By faith, Mary led the servants into following Jesus's instructions. It was this same faith that led her to believe that the wine deficit was a type of wrapping paper that needed to be removed for others to see him as living water flowing to fix a dry situation.

"Looking unto Jesus, the author and finisher of our faith" (Hebrews 12:2), makes all things possible regardless of what resources are available or any discouraging surrounding circumstances. "Jesus said to him, 'If you can believe, all things are possible to him who believes'" (Mark 9:23). Faith is the substance that looks for impossible situations often topped with discouraging surrounding circumstances. Often when an artist dreams or envisions a work, the creativity begins to take shape in their mind first before seeing how it will be constructed on paper. What can be most challenging for the artist is moving the dream or vision from a place of impossibilities surrounded with discouraging circumstance to a place of possibility. It is a leap of faith that many artists have to encounter when implementing their dreams or vision for others to see them in their concrete form. The artist's dream or vision is put together with raw materials or substance that looks nothing like the end result. However, these materials or substances are necessary in building the art piece into a reality for others to see what started as a dream or vision in the artist's mind. Faith is a substance often surrounded with discouraging circumstance; yet there is hope, for the artist brings their dreams and vision to a place of possibility.

God constantly looks for people to call on him when they face impossible situations or discouraging circumstances, knowing that he is the only one who can deliver them. As followers, we need to run out of wine to be better equipped believers. Faith is the way to hope. This mindset pleases God but allowing fear and doubt to undermine one's reaction toward impossible situations or discouraging circumstances does not please him. This was the day God broke the flow of water and used it to be Jesus's first recorded miracle by changing water into wine. "He that believeth on me, as the scripture hath said, out of his belly shall flow rivers of living water" (John 7:38 KJV). Mary came to know Jesus as the substance of her faith. Jesus was waiting for her faith to activate his first supernatural, recorded miracle. He saw through Mary's interactions among the servants that she believed the written word, and the living word is who Jesus is. Mary believed regardless of the timing or circumstance; she knew enough about who Jesus is and what the Scripture had said. Mary's part in the activation of this miracle came from what she believed about Jesus and what the Holy Spirit had instructed her concerning her role as the mother of Jesus. The wine today has run out, and as believers we are waiting for God to supply more wine, but it is God who is waiting for us to believe he is what the Scriptures have said and that he lives as the living word within us. How many people is God waiting for to trigger the things he has for them from the supernatural? "Now if God so clothes the grass of the field, which today is, and tomorrow is thrown into the oven, will He not much more clothe you, O you of little faith" (Matthew 6:30)?

The biggest barrier for some followers is their belief system as it relates to what the Scriptures say about who the son of God is. This is where revelation plays a huge role in understanding the things that believers find challenging. "The eyes of your understanding being enlightened; that ye may know what is the hope of his calling, and what the riches of the glory of his inheritance in the saints" (Ephesians 1:18 KJV). Jesus needs to be viewed as the substance of faith, often working as a silhouette in helping believers shape their perceptions through faith, using spiritual eyes. "No man hath seen God at any time" (John 1:18 KJV). God cannot be seen by natural sight, only through the substance of who Jesus is. Jesus is the way and the door to God, and he holds the discovery of what you were purposed for. During difficult circumstances, this is the day the Lord has made comes by revelation from God to help believers know and see who Jesus is. Rejoicing and being glad is having perfect peace in knowing who Jesus is because the son of God is in every type of day whether it is good, bad, or indifferent. In this case, rejoicing and being glad is led by the type of faith in which believers understand there is a purpose for every problem. Let us rejoice and be glad is an opportunity to say thank you to Jesus! The Lord is omniscient, knowing that, in time, things will work out for the good for those who love him and are called for his purpose. As followers, we serve a God who embedded in us the solutions for every problem or challenge, governed by the Holy Spirit. God has given to people as a father who gives to his children answers to questions, solutions to problems, antidotes to illnesses, and a shield for every weapon. God placed himself in a fatherly role, by supplying his children with the essential things in life, including the gifts that are within and the tools to remove the wrapping paper as part of the process in discovering one's purpose.

Faith does its best work when the storehouse is empty and the natural odds are against the believer. God the father, Jesus the son of God, and the Holy Spirit are always excited when all the right ingredients are present for faith to do its best work. In a perfect storm, the adversary often rides forcefully with dangerous waves. In the middle of a storm, Peter was walking on the water toward Jesus. An unexpected wind appeared, and Peter found himself sinking and screamed out for Jesus to save him. Understanding the substance of faith can be viewed like a bridge. The substance helps bring people closer to seeing Jesus in their thought process and not how they see him with their natural eyes. Jesus's mother, Mary, took her natural eyes off Jesus after she informed him of the wine shortage at the wedding party. When Mary turned toward the servants, she instructed them to do whatever Jesus said to do. This turning point for Mary was removing the wrapping paper in the process of Jesus's first noted miracle. Mary knew enough about faith that she did not have to limit herself by seeing Jesus as the son of God with her natural eyes but by using faith, which granted her access to know that all things are possible for those who believe. "But without faith it is impossible to please Him, for he who comes to God must believe that He is, and that He is a rewarder of those who diligently seek Him" (Hebrews 11:6).

Faith continues to work even against a stormy sea and in situations where all hope of bringing believers to a safe haven seems lost. Faith comes to believers not just by walking alongside them like a rod and staff, but also by preventing weapons from prospering and sometimes by being a life preserver to keep believers afloat until they are out of dangerous conditions. When Jesus told Peter that he had little faith, Jesus's intention was to illustrate that all things are possible in and by Jesus because he is the substance that makes what faith is. Regardless of how things are moving in life or in spite of the ups and downs in the process of discovering your purpose, faith is absolute in the thinking of believers. "With men this is impossible, but with God all things are possible" (Matthew 19:26).

Faith in Jesus is a type of conduit for getting things done from God. When you incorporate the mindset of Jesus, faith works as a medium for the desires of your heart to be revealed. "O, ye of little faith" can be understood based on how one sees Jesus in their thought process and not how he is perceived with the natural eye. It is not the size or quantity of one's faith needed to move a mountain, but it is in the quality of knowing who God is in both pleasant and unpleasant challenges.

A follower's belief system in God is rooted in a personal relationship with him through Jesus. In this relationship, followers look toward the substance of faith to govern their living, being, and movement. As people begin to remove the wrapping paper used in the process to cover their gifts, callings, or purpose, they become less dependent on what they see with their natural eyes.

The distance between this is the day the Lord has made and reaching toward rejoicing and being glad in it is the quality of faith one has in Jesus. Seek to know who Jesus is before the day begins, regardless of the type of day you are having or your ability to resolve struggles independently. It's this distance in reaching rejoicing and being glad where people often find themselves tripping with doubt. Bridging the distance requires a collaboration of faith and true worship. Jesus is the author of everything that takes place from the beginning of the day to the end of the day, and he is the source to rejoice and be glad in it. Because Jesus is the author of purpose, he has the power to create a new narrative, modify the story, or stand by what he has written concerning your destiny. His word gives people who love him and who are called the assurance that everything will work together for good according to his purpose: "And we know that all things work together for good to them that love God, to them who are the called according to his purpose" (Romans 8:28 KJV).

Jesus, our gift from God, is a living source of faith for believers. He is the substance of things hoped for and the evidence of things not seen. He will make room for purpose to take up residency in a believer's life and will order the necessary steps to succeed: "A man's gift makes room for him, and brings him before great men" (Proverbs 18:16). For believers to shine their gift in the presence of great people, faith requires work from them. The follower's work moves faith toward those things that are hoped for and for things to come into existence.

In making room for their gift, people need certain essentials, such as believing in who God says he is and believing that he is faithful in spite of how long it takes before one can operate in the purpose. This gift or purpose is intended not only to bless the individual but also to be a blessing to others and for God to get the glory. Making room for one gift is a process, which can take several days or up to many years before it reaches its ability to function in its purpose.

"For God so loved the world, that he gave his only begotten Son, that whosoever believeth in him should not perish, but have everlasting life" (John 3:16 KJV). Man's destiny before Jesus paid the price for our sins was based on the wages of sin, which is death; however, facts must submit to the truth. God is so loving and merciful that he sent his son in our place, and Jesus paid the debt in full as supporting evidence of the truth. This point illuminates who God is when a believer's faith is challenged: "But God, who is rich in mercy, for his great love wherewith he loved us" (Ephesians 2:4 KJV). Who God is and his love for the world overrule any circumstance, and his word and his presence become the truth over everything and anything. This gives believers reason to rejoice and be glad by simply knowing who God is.

One of the beauties of knowing God is to grasp that he "pre-gifts" individuals before they are born. Faith is one of the many gifts God gives, but it comes in a measured amount, according to his purpose and their destiny.

> For I say, through the grace given to me, to everyone who is among you, not to think of himself more highly than he ought to think, but to think soberly, as God has dealt to each one a measure of faith.
>
> —Rom. 12:3

Too often, people ask God for more faith when God is waiting for them to use the measure of faith he has already given them. It takes faith or a level of belief to receive what God has spoken or a promise he has given—including the measure of faith he has placed inside them. Some find it challenging to work the faith that has been given. Working the faith that God has already supplied means believing that what he has given you really works, regardless of the surrounding circumstance. "Do you see that faith was working together with his works, and by works faith was made perfect" (James 2:22)? God is waiting for people to do the work necessary to release the substance found in faith that creates the things we hope for. It is this supporting evidence of things we cannot see with our natural eye that becomes the source of energy, empowering the things we hope for. Hope in the process gives people the power to remove the wrapping paper in revealing their gift.

How faith works is similar to how yeast or leaven enhances the size of dough before it is baked. In this example, the dough represents people who work their faith like yeast to make the dough rise—the desire is to change an unfruitful situation into a rising and productive situation. Faith is what moves God to act on our behalf. "The kingdom of heaven is like leaven, which a woman took and hid in three measures of meal till it was all leavened" (Matthew 13:33). Faith, like yeast, is the substance of things hoped for, the evidence of things not seen. On special occasions, I bake yeast rolls for dinner. I buy the frozen dough already mixed with yeast. The process is time-consuming, but the end product is worth every bite. The process requires faith to collaborate with work. The work is in the preparation. The faith stems from believing that the instructions printed on the package will deliver awesome yeast rolls. The yeast used in the frozen dough cannot be seen by the naked eye. The consumer has to trust and believe that the unseen yeast exists and will provide the end results hoped for.

Like the yeast used in this example, faith cannot be seen by the naked eye. However, the set of instructions known as God's word will produce the thing that is hoped for when work collaborates with faith. Taking God at his word is an act of faith. This instructs believers to work toward a direction that appears unreliable to the naked eye. Moreover, believers who understand who God is have a place set aside in their thinking for his residency to govern their responses to uncertainties. God wants believers to face everything that the day brings with faith, even if the outcome appears uncertain. Think of believers as avid sports fans. God is their favorite sports team, and the game is the day the Lord has made. Committed fans share enthusiasm, respect, and love for their team that do not change with the score or who appears to be winning at any time. In the same way, devotion shared by true worshippers of God does not change because of challenges or problems faced. How does one get to the "let us rejoice and be glad in it" when facing adversities even when the adversary appears to be a giant? True worshippers, like committed sport fans, are often motivated when the going gets tough—even more so under pressure because it is the pressure that pushes them toward their destiny. It is this same pressure felt from adversities or challenges that sports fans and true worshippers are inspired to cheer, to praise, and to acknowledge in public that the one they are committed to is faithful!

In the Lord's prayer, Jesus instructs believers to ask God to give us this day our daily bread. "Delight yourself also in the LORD and He shall give you the desires of your heart" (Psalms 37:4). Despite your discomfort or lack of understanding, God has no intention of interrupting the process leading to your purpose. Nor will he allow any weapon to be formed to keep you from reaching your destiny. God is futuristic and spends little time in places of our uncertainty but rather finds rest in knowing who he is in our uncertainty. God is waiting for believers to find the place of rest with him, especially when they face worries, anxiety, and improbability. Finding that place of rest with Jesus empowers individuals to trust in who Jesus is rather than in worries or anxiety. The relationship between believers and God was never about our might, but about the strength that comes from knowing who Jesus is. Moreover, building an intimate relationship with Jesus is one of the greatest gifts one can give him. "For God so loved the world that He gave His only begotten Son, that whoever believes in Him should not perish but have everlasting life" (John 3:16). Therefore, people should stop depending totally on religious activities as a way to God but rather as a way to open and develop a personal relationship with God. The hunger of individuals who desire a personal, intimate relationship draws them into his presence and to the place of rest.

Mary, Jesus's mother, could tap into the power of who Jesus is by expanding her relationship with Jesus beyond that of being his mother. Through the Holy Spirit, God empowered Mary to tap into a faith that could be activated only through Jesus. This activation can occur only with a personal yet intimate relationship with God through Jesus. This same power of faith is available for people today through developing a personal, intimate relationship with God through Jesus.

> *No man shall be able to stand before you all the days of your life; as I was with Moses, so I will be with you. I will not leave you nor forsake you. Be strong and of good courage, for to this people you shall divide as an inheritance the land which I swore to their fathers to give them. Only be strong and very courageous.*
>
> —Josh. 1:5–7

Especially during days when you need courage and encouragement, find comfort in knowing that the God who was with the forefathers is the same God with followers today.

Jesus turning the wine into water was most significant as it was his first noted miracle. For the wedding party, it became an unexpected blessing. However, Mary's mindset as a believer illustrated the essential role she had in the miracle. She spoke to the substance of who Jesus is from her heart in spite of natural limitations and barriers. Up to this moment, Mary kept many things concerning who Jesus is hidden in her heart. But that day, she removed the wrapping paper by speaking from her heart and out of her belly came rivers of living water. "He that believeth on me, as the scripture hath said, out of his belly shall flow rivers of living water" (John 7:38 KJV). Mary did not let the situation and limited physical resources dictate her response of who Jesus is. Her thinking empowered her to rejoice and be glad in the day the Lord has made. The woman at the well, Jesus's mother, and Mary who anointed the Lord with fragrant oil and wiped his feet with her hair shared one particular thing associated with Jesus. They were exposed to who he is, and as a result of their belief, rivers of living water began to flow out of their bellies.

God has given the power of Jesus Christ through the Holy Spirit to operate inside people to do even greater works than he did.

Most assuredly, I say to you, he who believes in Me, the works that I do he will do also; and greater works than these he will do, because I go to My Father. And whatever you ask in My name, that I will do, that the Father may be glorified in the Son. If you ask anything in My name, I will do it.

—John 14:12–14

Activation of the substance of faith is best done when faced with challenges that come out of nowhere and in places where hope appears futile.

Having a close personal relationship with Jesus can turn unexpected challenges into a gift from God where he will make room in the minds of believers for a state of rejoicing and being glad in the one who made the day. This doesn't limit followers to always feeling glad but being glad because, like Mary, believers know who Jesus is. God made room by increasing the territory in Mary's mind and womb by being Jesus's mother, but more so in her mindset as a worshipper because she knew who God is, in spirit and in truth. Every day that God gives is a gift from him. Although the days may be filled with uncertainty, there is a promise for every uncertainty. In some seasons, God increases territory for his seeds of greatness to reach their full potential and productivity in the life of people.

"Come to Me, all you who labor and are heavy laden, and I will give you rest" (Matthew 11:28). A resting place as it relates to removing the wrapping paper in the process of revealing your gift or purpose provides a sense of peace knowing who you are and that the purpose you serve in life is found in I Am. God, who is known as I Am, uses the Holy Spirit to empower individuals to remove the wrapping paper in the process. As the territory of discovering who you are in I Am comes closer, a resting place by faith is produced where people place their trust in God in spite of the challenges of removing the wrapping paper used for the process. Trust becomes a resting place for mature believers during this expansion of territory. God creates or expands the territory for some to further develop; this part of the process gets uncomfortable. For faith to be fruitful, it must be in a place where emptiness has taken up residency. Work becomes an opportunity to create something out of nothing. This is the day the Lord has made is an opportunity for believers to rest in any day that God has given, knowing there is more than enough grace to supply their daily needs, but most of all believing they are more like I Am than they think. God will make room for Jesus as a measure of faith so that people can discover who they are as it relates to purpose.

This resting place that only Jesus can provide gives the ability to operate daily in their purpose regardless of areas of deficits, adversities, or overly anxious feelings in unwrapping the paper for the process. "Therefore submit to God. Resist the devil and he will flee from you" (James 4:7). To resist the devil is to overcome the feelings of being overly anxious while removing the wrapping paper for process. There is a noted distance in reaching rejoicing and being glad from this is the day that the Lord has made as one begins to remove the wrapping paper for the process. However, it is this distance in the process that provides important learning moments designed to empower people to effectively maintain the function of their purpose. Being overly anxious toward the type of wrapping paper used to cover the gift God gives you comes from the carnality of our mind. Adversities and the adversary can increase believers' levels of anxiety and distract them from the process of obtaining their gift. Keeping your mind and spiritual eyes on the prize and not placing your focus on the wrapping paper will make the adversary leave. Rejoicing and being glad in the day that the Lord begins by having the same mindset that is in Jesus now in you.

> For to be carnally minded is death, but to be spiritually minded is life and peace. Because the carnal mind is enmity against God; for it is not subject to the law of God, nor indeed can be. So then, those who are in the flesh cannot please God.
>
> —Rom. 8:6–8

When people submit to God, it becomes their new normal of seeing. While unwrapping the paper in the process, this new mindset or seeing things through Jesus's eyes shortens the distance to realizing this is the day the Lord has made. Rejoicing and being glad in the process of knowing God and the purpose he has for you lead to knowing that the struggle was worth it. This is day that the Lord has made is a process that one has to go through to unwrap who they are to live their purpose. Nevertheless, the process to live life with purpose can be a struggle, including the struggle that comes with the calling in suiting up for destiny.

CALLED TO
SUIT UP

CHAPTER 2

Often people are required to wear a suit that makes it easy for others to identify the function, position, and calling associated with their purpose. Superman, a well-known superhero, wore a suit as Clark Kent to cover up his true identity. The suit that covered up Superman was the role of Clark Kent, a journalist for *The Daily Planet*. Needless to say, the suit worn by Clark Kent covered Superman's true identity as one who was created to improve the world by fighting crime. Too often, people choose to wear a suit of doubt, fear, anxiety, and uncertainty to hide who they really are in God's eyes by not living their purpose. Sometimes, a suit is used as an undercover to hide a person's purpose to avoid making a difference in the world prematurely. In the process of discovering and living one's purpose, it is worth the struggle of learning how to suit up for the appointed time. Challenges or problems are keys often used as turning points in suiting up. At times, it is these turning points that call people to be pushed into their true identities. Inside every purpose placed in a person is a solution attached to attract the problem or problems they were destined to solve. The suiting up component of the struggle is worth it because it empowers individuals to move from knowledge to wisdom. The focus on discovering purpose should have a short life span, whereas the focus on living the purpose God placed within us is continuous. The discovery component provides knowledge that you have a purpose; however, it is wisdom that teaches how to live life on purpose.

When my mother was 85 years old and working full time, she asked me to drive her from Washington, DC, to New York for the fourth consecutive year after she attended The National Association of Community Health Centers Conference (NACHC). Each year, she asked me to pick her up in Washington, DC, and drive her home to Peekskill, New York. In those four years, I did what my mother asked me with a smile and a servant mindset because of who she is in my life. I never told my mother that I hated driving to Washington, DC, for several sound reasons. What I hated most was the fear of getting lost. Several days before picking up my mother, I found it hard to fall asleep at night because I allowed fear and anxiety to overcome me. What if I make the wrong turn or miss the right turn? I entertained every imaginable thing that could go wrong. I began to consider alternatives I could offer my mother as a way for her to get home other than getting a ride with me. So many alternatives popped into my head as I kept weighing her call to which I had said yes.

> *(For the weapons of our warfare are not carnal, but mighty through God to the pulling down of strongholds;) casting down imaginations, and every high thing that exalteth itself against the knowledge of God, and bringing into captivity every thought to the obedience of Christ.*
>
> —2 Cor. 10:4–5 KJV

God spoke to my fears by asking me a question: "In the past four years, have you ever gotten so lost that you were not able to pick up your mother and bring her home safely and do so with a sound mind?" My response to God was never! And then God asked me with something like, "Why would you waste the energy I gave you to invest in fear instead of investing in the spirit that gives you power to overcome and a sound mind to answer the call to suit up?" Scripture says, "For God has not given us a spirit of fear, but of power and of love and of a sound mind" (2 Timothy 1:7). I had to put my fears aside and believe in who God is in my times of uncertainty.

Believing in God's word often begins in prayer or speaking with God and not to him. The art of speaking with God comes from having a mindset like Jesus, which fosters a transformed thought process that empowers individuals to have a conversation with him. This conversation carries a promise that lives and moves in strategic steps to prepare followers to do what God has spoken into existence concerning their purpose. Rejoicing and being glad stems from knowing the God who placed the call to the chosen and from understanding that he placed the call with a purpose. He backs up every call, knowing it will go through as he said it would. Because he is omniscient, the call will be answered with purpose on the receiving end. The chosen are those who God knows will answer his call for the sake of purpose and by the way of process: "My sheep hear My voice, and I know them, and they follow Me" (John 10:27).

> God called to him from the midst of the bush and said, "Moses, Moses!" And he said, "Here I am." Then He said, "Do not draw near this place. Take your sandals off your feet, for the place where you stand is holy ground." Moreover, He said, "I am the God of your father—the God of Abraham, the God of Isaac, and the God of Jacob."
>
> —Exod. 3:4–6

Elsewhere in the Bible, Noah was called to suit up when God instructed him to do something never done before based on something he had never seen before. God instructed Noah to act on faith. That call to action led him to his destiny. Mary used an expensive perfumed ointment kept in a closed alabaster box. Her calling was to help facilitate Jesus's destiny as the one who is the resurrection and the life. This Mary whose brother was Lazarus, a close friend of Jesus, used the expensive perfumed ointment on Jesus and wiped his feet with her hair after anointing them with the ointment. It wasn't until the box was broken that the ointment and its aroma could do its purpose, which was to aid in worshipping Jesus. Mary played an important role, though it was considered small in the eyes of those who saw what she did for Jesus. "For who has despised the day of small things" (Zechariah 4:10)? What appear to be small things or several slow changes in the process will soon be worth the struggle. "Assuredly, I say to you, wherever this gospel is preached in the whole world, what this woman has done will also be told as a memorial to her" (Matthew 26:13).

Each day relates to "this is the day that the Lord has made" and is part of a process for individuals to live in their purpose. Do not become frustrated in the workroom where purpose is being developed. God uses various types of workrooms as spiritual darkrooms where the seed can develop to become fruitful. Some places that are used as workrooms include our jobs, homes, churches, and relationships. Moreover, present, past, and future learning experiences are also used in workrooms to teach and promote people to live in their calling or purpose A workplace used as a spiritual darkroom is similar to an art studio where God arranges and rearranges gifts for the sake of purpose. A spiritual darkroom is used to prepare people to become supernaturally effective in their purpose on earth. The spiritual darkroom is not the place where your gift originates, but the darkroom is where it is shaped for purpose. The spiritual darkroom prepares individuals by further developing their faith over adversities or challenges. Others' need of your gift makes room for your purpose to be very effective. For example, the purpose of having sliced bread served as a wonderful change in preparing meals more effectively for many people throughout the world. Your gift is a solution to man's challenge; nevertheless, fulfilling your purpose is a process often consisting of barriers that stand in the way of reaching what you were purposed to do or the call for which you are better suited.

The workplace in a spiritual darkroom, and the barriers you have to remove or go through are very small compared to the room your gift has made for you and your purpose. "A man's gift makes room for him and brings him before great men" (Proverbs 18:16). Various events and steps bring destiny to the appointed time for people to reach their purpose. Walking toward rejoicing and being glad in the process fosters a level of faith that believers have in their worship of God. The relationship between believers and God becomes more personal and intimate as the appointed time meets up with their destiny. During the developmental stages, a little fertilizer will facilitate faith in reaching destiny. "Seek first the kingdom of God" was intended for believers to discover the substance of who God is and to avoid getting hung up on religion. And by understanding the substance of faith, believers discover their true identity. Many people are familiar with the word *faith*, but in the process of personal spiritual development, the substance of faith needs to be examined.

> *Now faith is the substance of things hoped for, the evidence of things not seen. For by it the elders obtained a good report. Through faith we understand that the worlds were framed by the word of God, so that things which are seen were not made of things which do appear.*
>
> —Heb. 11:1–3 KJV

When a seed is planted in fertilized soil, it is framed by everything it needs to produce fruit. Similarly, after conception has taken place in the womb, the human egg is framed with everything its needs to develop into a living human being. God used his faith as fertilizer to frame our destiny.

Fertilizer promotes the growth and the development of plant life. Dark, moist, earthy soil can be difficult to distinguish from fertilizer. As it relates to faith, fertilizer is the substance that frames seeds and often works in places where darkness surrounds hope. People who use this substance will find that a fruitful plant will sprout in spite of its current nonexistence. When consumers use fertilizer, they take a leap of faith that the substance inside the bag will live up to the manufacturer's promise. Consumers are hoping for something that cannot be seen. Advertisements about the fertilizer contain facts about how it supports growth, but what's inside the bag is where truth lives and can make a difference. Consumers expect to produce a plant that in time will be fruitful. For believers, understanding the substance of faith is needed to obtain what is being hoped for. Fertilizer, like faith, requires something in collaboration with it to succeed.

> *But someone will say, "You have faith, and I have works."*
> *Show me your faith without your works, and I will show you*
> *my faith by my works. You believe that there is one God. You do*
> *well. Even the demons believe—and tremble! But do you want*
> *to know, O foolish man, that faith without works is dead?*
>
> —James 2:18–20

For believers, different types of soil can challenge their "planting season." In other words, different types of circumstances in life can challenge believers in stages of growth and development. Adversities can appear in the environment or mind at any time. Having the mindset necessary to till the fields and develop the faith requires believers to change the way they think about the expected results from the "fertilizer" alone. Work is needed. Using faith alone will not produce the result hoped for.

With plants, water is an essential element for growth and productivity. "He who believes in Me, as the Scripture has said, out of his heart will flow rivers of living water" (John 7:38). This water that flows from worship activates the nutrients in the fertilizer or faith to stimulate hope, and the focus is no longer on the challenges or adversities from the earthly soil. That thing the consumer or believer has been hoping for provides God the platform to make it grow. "I have planted, Apollos watered; but God gave the increase" (1 Corinthians 3:6 KJV). God gives seeds of greatness to believers. The challenge for people is discovering what God placed inside the shell of the seeds. God gives a measure of faith to every believer in the seeds of greatness. However, to bring the seeds to fruition, the seed's shell must be broken. Breaking the shell is where transformation begins. A call to action moves believers to seek a deeper and a much more personal relationship with God through Jesus. Faith is best developed in a believer when it is perceived as a living substance created by God to help followers understand who they are and how they move in spiritual darkrooms. Faith as a living substance is not a concept, an idea, positive thinking, or food for thought. Rather, it flows like a river of living substance that moves with purpose. "For as the body without the spirit is dead, so faith without works is dead also" (James 2:26). Because God is omniscient, he knew that the only way faith could work was for it to exist as a living substance, not embedded in a good idea that is not destined to take flight.

"For everyone to whom much is given, from him much will be required; and to whom much has been committed, of him they will ask the more" (Luke 12:48). When God gives his seeds of greatness, a clause is attached. God has a higher level of expectation for people who are chosen and called into action. Seeds of greatness require work to take root and become fruitful. The necessary work can be challenging and, to some, even discouraging. Faith is an essential tool in the groundbreaking process to create a place for planting and watering and accelerating growth. However, faith is at its best when God accelerates that thing into abundance from a place where life did not exist before. Because God is omnipresent, he is involved throughout the process of an individual getting to know who God is. In addition, his revelation becomes obtainable because of his faithfulness. God is so faithful to his seeds of greatness that his word will have the last say. Still, he waits for followers to believe in him, to take him fully at his word, and to believe that he is faithful to his seeds. To believers who are called into action, God is faithful because he allows the growth of his seeds of greatness:

> *So then neither is he that planteth any thing, neither he that watereth; but God that giveth the increase. Now he that planteth and he that watereth are one: and every man shall receive his own reward according to his own labour.*
>
> —1 Cor. 3:7–8 KJV

Faith comes by hearing the word of God. The word of God is the substance of who Jesus is—the substance of the things not seen and the evidence of things hoped for. I remember going to my mother when I was in my last trimester of pregnancy after experiencing Braxton-Hicks contractions for several weeks. I asked her to look at me and tell me whether she thought I was in my labor process. For days, she would say, "Althea, you are not ready to have this baby yet." Disappointed in her response, I would ask her, "How do you know that I am not ready yet?" She would simply tell me, "Because you don't look ready yet." I asked my mother what I must look like for her to know that I was ready to go into labor. She said you need to look worn out and tired. She went on to say, "Right now, you look too good, your hair is well-groomed, and you look too rested." I depended on my mother's intuition as a gauge for how close I was to going into labor. At times, pregnant women can become frustrated in the labor process, just like followers who are pregnant with destiny can become frustrated in the process. God used my mother's intuition, similar to the role of the Holy Spirit, to let me know when my appointed time would come for labor and the birthing of my gift or purpose. The Holy Spirit as a comforter and, in many cases, as a midwife works to facilitate the process of delivery for the anointed at the appointed time. As a young, married pregnant woman, I learned to trust my mother's intuition; although, there were times I truly believed I was ready to go into labor. The feelings I had with waiting for labor and delivery were similar to the waiting I went through for my anointing to catch up with my appointed time. I simply had to learn to trust the Holy Spirit for the appointed time just as I had to learn to trust my mother's intuition for the delivery time.

Faith empowers believers to trust God when it looks like he cannot be found and hope seems nonexistent. In the midst of an unexpected storm in life, faith is the ability to trust Jesus and believe that things will work out for the good. Faith is that bridge that connects the impossible to mission possible. The substance of faith cannot be seen with the natural eye or by the carnality of the human mind. The pure substance of faith is knowing the core of who Jesus is by way of revelation. Revelation is a gift from God that empowers people by disclosing his thoughts to foster a better understanding of his plans. People often gauge the outcome of each day based on the type of day they are experiencing rather than knowing the core of God as the source of having perfect peace in spite of what the day may bring. "You will keep him in perfect peace, whose mind is stayed on You, because he trusts in You" (Isaiah 26:3). Knowing who he is gives perfect peace in responding to daily struggles. Trust Jesus, the pure substance of faith. In doing so, this will keep your mind on him. God did not create this day without preparing all the things that would take place, including the Holy Spirit living inside believers to strengthen individuals' ability to cope with difficulty. When God creates a day, he takes into consideration the people first because he loves them, and he is faithful in his word.

> *For God so loved the world that He gave His only begotten Son, that whoever believes in Him should not perish but have everlasting life. For God did not send His Son into the world to condemn the world, but that the world through Him might be saved.*
>
> —John 3:16–17

Every day God instructs believers to rejoice and be glad in every situation. Rejoicing and being glad in the day the Lord has made doesn't always mean wearing a smile on your face when confronted with adversity. God wants people to worship who he is when the sun shines and during a storm. We are to worship him simply because he made the day regardless of the struggle we're facing in the moment. We learn to rejoice and be glad in the day he has made because struggles are sent in the process to propel people to succeed in their purpose. God is I Am, and he is everything people need. This is the day the Lord has made is about seeking the kingdom of God by way of knowing you were made right to live your purpose as he has planned. In the day the Lord has made, God has granted access to his ways and thoughts for everyone in their pursuit of the kingdom to have an abundant life through purpose. As people seek first the kingdom of God and its righteousness, they will come to know and believe that the plans that God has pertaining to their purpose are guaranteed to succeed. The kingdom of heaven holds the truth of everyone's identity concerning their purpose. The journey of seeking first the kingdom of God provides the wisdom necessary to live life with purpose, and in due season, people will come to know the struggle they went through was worth it to live their life on purpose.

In John 14:6 (NIV), "Jesus answered, 'I am the way and the truth and the life. No one comes to the Father except through me.'" Walking by faith and not by sight is the opportunity to have Jesus as a friend who is the author and finisher of faith and who just happens to have a pencil with an eraser ready if needed to write a new narrative.

People are led by the Holy Spirit in living out their purpose. Revelation, relationship, faith, and a transformed mindset empower people to worship God. When walking in Jesus, it is by faith and not by sight. Walking in Jesus is not walking with him or being at his side. It's having a mindset that elevates followers to think like him. People who become followers of God's ways and thoughts are led to a place where they can rejoice even though they wonder at times why God made this day. "'For My thoughts are not your thoughts, nor are your ways My ways,' says the Lord. 'For as the heavens are higher than the earth, so are My ways higher than your ways, and My thoughts than your thoughts'" (Isaiah 55:8–9). A transformed mindset changes your conversation from talking to God to talking with God. Being Jesus-like-minded gives people access to God's ways and thoughts. In the process, you will find answers to questions concerning your purpose, why you were chosen, the thing that makes you different from others, why you feel apart from others, and why others can't see your true identity. It's unfortunate that only a few will leave the altar call of salvation and be about purpose; nevertheless, the invitation to seek the kingdom of heaven is extended to everyone. This is the day the Lord has made is about seeking one's purpose in a spiritual darkroom prepared by God to develop and cultivate one's destiny. Purpose gives people a reason not just to live, but it motivates individuals to live more abundantly in their personal relationship with God. The call to be chosen is often paired with adversities. Consequently, adversities are opportunities for God to show up and to show out his faithfulness. God is faithful in each day. The rejoicing and being glad in it is a response to what he has already done. This new way of thinking helps to shorten the distance between the time of anointing and the time of appointment and, for most people, it lessens levels of anxiety when faced with doubt.

In my kitchen, I have a cabinet that stores many different types of containers, each designed to hold a certain amount of food for future use. To the average person, my cabinet looks like a hot mess. When I need to find a specific container, I pull out every one, if necessary, to find the container that fulfills the job, and then I place the rest back in the cabinet for future use. Like my containers, God often chooses people who appear to be surrounded by a hot mess in an environment with other people of different shapes, sizes, colors, and purposes. As people in the process of living life on purpose, we need to learn to trust God in what often appears to be a hot mess in our immediate environment and see an opportunity for God to unveil a masterpiece—at his appointed time. Every container in my cabinet was purchased to fill a specific purpose although every container has not yet fulfilled its purpose. An appointed time is a destined time when a vessel or container is filled by the Holy Spirit to do a specific job that it was created to do. When the appointed time arrives, the container will not have to change its size or shape to fulfill its calling. Every container purchased was called beforehand to fulfill its purpose at the appointed time. Like most containers or vessels, people have a future purpose, which God has given that only they can fulfill because they are the right size, shape, and color for the job. In my cabinet, I have used some containers more frequently than others, yet there's not one that I am willing to discard. Each one was called, chosen, and purchased to serve a purpose. "But we have this treasure in earthen vessels, that the excellence of the power may be of God and not of us. We are hard-pressed on every side, yet not crushed; we are perplexed, but not in despair" (2 Corinthians 4:7–8).

Most typical days that the Lord has made are not quite a walk in the park, but more like faith walking on the water:

> *Shortly before dawn Jesus went out to them, walking on the lake. When the disciples saw him walking on the lake, they were terrified. "It's a ghost," they said, and cried out in fear. But Jesus immediately said to them: "Take courage! It is I. Don't be afraid." "Lord, if it's you," Peter replied, "tell me to come to you on the water." "Come," he said. Then Peter got down out of the boat, walked on the water and came toward Jesus. But when he saw the wind, he was afraid and, beginning to sink, cried out, "Lord, save me!" Immediately Jesus reached out his hand and caught him. "You of little faith," he said, "why did you doubt?" And when they climbed into the boat, the wind died down. Then those who were in the boat worshipped him, saying, "Truly you are the Son of God."*
>
> —Matt. 14:25–33 NIV

Faith cannot be seen with the naked eye, and doubts have no place in what God has announced. "Even though I walk through the valley of the shadow of death, I will fear no evil, for you are with me; your rod and your staff, they comfort me" (Psalm 23:4 ESV). Rejoicing and being glad comes from understanding who Jesus is and the influence he has on each day concerning your purpose. "For we walk by faith, not by sight" (2 Corinthians 5:7). Faith comes from hearing the words that Jesus speaks. These words give life over every situation people face daily. Hearing fosters faith as you trust what the Scripture says you are. Follow Jesus, who is God's word sent from heaven as the evidence of things hoped for.

The pathway to what God has designed is often littered with fear and doubt, which followers experience on the journey to their destiny. Nevertheless, the pathway cultivates faith in followers as they tackle the scary moments. Fear can discourage, yet it is necessary at times to provide the evidence needed to believe. Jesus walks ahead of us, and the Holy

Spirit is sent to comfort and empower us. The fearful places collaborate with faith to develop the purpose grafted into who you are and come with the intent to be witnessed for the glory of God. Jesus, the author of every story, can best describe a person's true identity, and he has the power to physically move, change, increase, alter, or influence challenging circumstances to empower people to succeed in reaching their purpose. To understand the substance of faith is to understand the meaning of a paradoxical image such that you can look at one thing and see something totally different. This ability is based on personal perception. People in search of their destiny often find themselves looking at the process as a paradoxical image. Do not depend on current or past perception of your life experiences in pursuing your purpose. As you delve more closely into the pursuit of purpose, your perception may change, and as a result, you will see something you did not see before. In pursuit of purpose, you may initially view religion as the way to know who God is and not see that the key to purpose is having a personal relationship with Jesus. Religion does not expose people to their true identity, but knowing Jesus through a personal relationship does. Jesus is the best mirror anyone could ever have to see how purpose should look. He is everything that's desirable in the heart of others as he waits for them at the peak of discovering their true identity. Greater is he who is in you than he who is in the world, including all types of mental disorders and the cultural diversity that often cause internal and external conflict among people. God's love removes all barriers, veils, walls, and surfaces that separate people from getting to the true substance of who Jesus is. Whereas other substances used in a form of abuse become ineffective coping skills in the struggle of living life on purpose, it is helpful to realize that the struggle was never intended to be with you forever. Rather, the struggle is a walk of faith in the process that leads you to their destiny. Having faith before seeing the victory makes the struggle worth it.

The process of knowing the substance of who Jesus is and knowing who you are as a believer in him is an inside job led by the Holy Spirit. The Holy Spirit leads you toward understanding the substance of your faith and who you are as a believer in Jesus. Understanding the substance of faith holds much weight in getting to the core of who Jesus is. Jesus once asked his followers:

> *"But who do you say that I am?" Simon Peter answered and said, "You are the Christ, the Son of the living God." Jesus answered and said to him, "Blessed are you, Simon Bar-Jonah, for flesh and blood has not revealed this to you, but My Father who is in heaven. And I also say to you that you are Peter, and on this rock, I will build My church, and the gates of Hades shall not prevail against it. And I will give you the keys of the kingdom of heaven, and whatever you bind on earth will be bound in heaven, and whatever you loose on earth will be loosed in heaven." Then He commanded His disciples that they should tell no one that He was Jesus the Christ.*
>
> —Matt. 16:15–21

The substance of faith as it relates to knowing Jesus is always much deeper than how life appears on the surface. Challenging situations are used as a type of wrapping paper to cover your purpose and to distract you from pursuing your true identity as it relates to your purpose. However, some individuals will dig deeper, removing the wrapping paper because they know there has to be something so much more beyond the challenges associated with discovering their purpose. Walking with Jesus encourages followers to speak with Jesus rather than speaking to him. Speaking to God often communicates misconceptions about the past that discourage some from seeking their destiny. Speaking to God focuses more on the facts and not the truth of how God sees you as his beloved child. Speaking with God places truth as the key component in your conversation. Truth bears much more weight than the facts presented in any case. The facts against man are stacked so high. But the truth of who God is empowered love to raise up against every fact that supported man's sinful disconnect from God. The truth spoke grace and mercy by proving its case: God so loved the world that he gave his only begotten son, which overruled every fact noted against man.

Truth is the very thing required to worship God in spirit. Worshipping God speaks to the things that are true about God. Facts are overruled by his truth consistently as demonstrated by his love found in his word and inscribed in his faithfulness. True worshippers speak the truth about God regardless of the facts presented, which appear to be piling up against his favor and against all odds. Believers are called to action to learn how to worship God in spirit and in truth. To worship God in spirit is to know him through revelation and by his Spirit as your guide to all truth. "The Spirit of truth, whom the world cannot receive, because it neither sees Him nor knows Him; but you know Him, for He dwells with you and will be in you" (John 14:17).

Anyone can become great in the power of God by the Holy Spirit. People who know their purpose in life are not just called by their given name from their parents, but their name takes on a whole new meaning concerning their purpose. God informed Abram that he had a new purpose:

> *I will make you a great nation; I will bless you and make your name great; and you shall be a blessing. I will bless those who bless you, and I will curse him who curses you; and in you all the families of the earth shall be blessed.*
>
> —Gen. 12:2–3

Doors open because of the power behind the name and the substance in the name that gives it power. Jesus asked, "Who do men say the son of God is?" The answer to this question is located deep in the core of who Jesus is as revealed by the power of the Holy Spirit. God told Moses to tell the Israelites that his name is I Am; he is the substance that contains everything they hope for and the evidence of things not seen. God provides many roads and paths to get to the substance of who Jesus is so that seekers can discover that substance and not just his name. The key to understanding faith is not by getting a superficial meaning of what faith is, but by embracing its substance. The substance of faith comes from believing in the core of who Jesus is. This is where our natural eyesight serves no purpose in witnessing what he can do. The core of who he is empowers others to spring forth rivers of living water in a place where life never existed. Faith flourishes best in an environment where people have nothing in their hands to create what they desire. Believe in the power of Jesus according to who he is and as the one who can make what you desire come to fruition. As the copilot of your destiny, you have the power to change your narrative by allowing the Holy Spirit to become your pilot or representative of your true identity.

What are the things in your life that represent you when someone speaks your purpose? People often get stuck in what they went through until they realize that their misfortunes or perceived mistakes were opportunities for learning to take place, advancing them toward their destiny. People tend to put so much focus on the journey or in the process rather than realizing that their purpose is so much greater than what they had to go through in arriving at their destiny. This is one of the reasons why God instructs people to rejoice and be glad in the day he has made, because the purpose is greater than the journey. This is true even though the process is a necessary part of reaching your purpose. When periods of frustration and uncertainty arise, worship the one who promised that you were created with purpose. At different points in my journey of understanding my purpose, I would pray, "Father God, open my eyes of understanding as it relates to how I think that I may see you in times where I question whether anything good can come out of the struggle."

CAN ANYTHING GOOD COME FROM A NEGATIVE?

CHAPTER 3

Jesus, the author and finisher of our faith, is the prerequisite of things hoped for and the proof of things before they appear. One of the biggest challenges in the journey of seeking the kingdom of God is the process of finding one's purpose. The eagerness to become what God has revealed to them as the finished project empowers people, yet God starts them from the beginning using the Holy Spirit to guide them to their appointed time. "Declaring the end from the beginning, and from ancient times things that are not yet done, saying, 'My counsel shall stand, and I will do all My pleasure'" (Isaiah 46:10). The steps are preordered to help believers develop their faith while cultivating their ability to hope for things they cannot see with their natural eyes. Struggle is part of the process that the Lord has made for followers to work through their purpose.

In this journey, followers learn to trust God, and worship becomes an effective coping skill against challenges. For followers to be successful in the process, they must have the same mindset as Jesus. This mindset reassures believers that Jesus controls all spiritual darkrooms, which serve as places where lessons are learned for future development of purpose. The dictionary best describes a darkroom as a room that can be made totally dark to permit the processing of the light-sensitive photographic materials, involving film, photographic paper, enlargers, running water, and baths mixed with special chemicals. Spiritual darkrooms are areas in a believer's thought process where the old mindset changes to a new way of thinking through life experiences as they search for the kingdom of God. "And be not conformed to this world: but be ye transformed by the renewing of your mind, that ye may prove what is that good, and acceptable, and perfect, will of God" (Romans 12:2 KJV). This new mindset is prearranged in the transformation process. Before entering a spiritual darkroom, followers must first be empty of all opinions of what they think they should be as a finished product concerning the plans of God. This new way of thinking provides Jesus with a blank sheet of photographic paper onto which a follower's true identity is exposed.

"For who hath despised the day of small things? for they shall rejoice" (Zechariah 4:10 KJV). When my mother started teaching me how to cook, I learned from sitting in a chair and watching her prepare the family meals, watching the steps that led to the finished product. The process she used did not always make a lot of sense to me. She took numerous steps to ensure that her dishes would turn out perfectly delicious. My mother believed that allowing me to observe the process would be more beneficial for teaching me how to cook than reading a recipe. She believed that if I learned and mastered the process, the end product would taste, look, and turn out perfectly delicious, just like hers. It wasn't until I matured spiritually in my relationship with God through Jesus that I learned the way a process gives rise to a greater appreciation of doing things God's way. As believers, appreciating the process fosters trust in the steps preordered from God. Feeling anxious about where you are in the process goes against the mindset of Christ Jesus and the thoughts he has about your purpose. This type of mindset affects how people trust God and the steps he has ordered in the process to expose them to their destiny. When believers feel anxious or worried about the process, submitting to who God is will turn worry into worship.

To really appreciate the process is to understand it as a form of worship in which we glorify God by trusting in who he is and what he has established concerning our purpose. God used my cooking experiences with my mother to help me to appreciate the process involved in preparing food to taste delicious and to better understand the process in discovering one's purpose. The experiences also helped me understand how important it is to rejoice and to be glad in the day the Lord has made before the finished product. Faith, in the process of discovering purpose, brings followers closer to God by having a personal, intimate relationship with Jesus. "But without faith it is impossible to please Him, for he who comes to God must believe that He is, and that He is a rewarder of those who diligently seek Him" (Hebrews 11:6).

One of the key components that led me to become the cook I am today was through developing a personal, intimate relationship with food. As I learned to cook with my mother, I developed a personal relationship with food by tasting the mixture and the different ingredients she added for taste and by seeing the different types of tools she used to transform the mixture until the dish reached its final presentation. My mother taught me to cook by faith and not by reading a recipe. I learned how to cook simply by tasting her work throughout the process, including the bitter and the sweet. As I improved as a cook, my mother was better able to judge my advanced level of cooking based on the dish's taste and presentation. Using the example of baking a homemade apple pie, my mother would let me taste the mixture throughout the process. Experiencing how the food tasted during the process was not just to teach me how to make a homemade apple pie but also how faith, work, precision, time, certain ingredients, the right tools, experience, and a working oven can change or transform raw material into something extraordinarily delicious. Needless to say, God used this life experience with my mother to illustrate to me how the steps in the process of reaching purpose can create a better appreciation for why people should rejoice and be glad in the process of this is the day the Lord has made.

This new appreciation or mindset of discovering one's true identity or purpose in the day the Lord has made provides people with living life with purpose. Many homemade fruit pastries consist of ingredients such as a measure of fresh-squeezed lemon juice, seasonal fruit, dark brown sugar, nutmeg, cinnamon, salt, pure vanilla extract, flour, cold water, shortening, and butter. If eaten or drunk separately, these ingredients could leave an undesirable taste or an unwanted experience. Each step in making the pie is necessary to arrive at the desired outcome. As in pie preparation, every step is crucial in the day of process that the Lord has made. Although it can be challenging at times, rejoice and be glad in every step taken toward purpose. Even when the steps toward destiny fail to resemble the finished product, rejoicing and being glad is a requirement that can only be done by faith.

Most people would not volunteer to enter into a heated oven for any period of time, especially knowing that the only way to come out of the oven is dependent on someone opening the door from the outside. Although an oven is a place that generates heat, it is essential for baking an apple pie. Just as it is essential to enter and leave the spiritual darkroom, one must learn to trust God in the process. Stepping into a spiritual darkroom where adversities are used to develop the best picture of who you can become is uncomfortable.

Followers come to accept that God is in control and that he knows how much time the pie requires in the oven or how much time a believer needs in a spiritual darkroom for the end product to be finished and ready for purpose. As I watched my mother bake pies, I learned that no pie takes the exact same number of minutes in the oven as another. When I reflect on the different types of pies she baked, certain variables played a role in determining the amount of time each pie needed to be in the oven. My mother took into consideration each variable, such as whether the pie was in a deep dish or the type of raw apples she used or whether she used a double pie crust or a single crust with a crumb top. After taking everything into consideration, she would determine the temperature to preheat the oven before baking, and then she would adjust the temperature to bake the pie. In the this-is-the-day-of process, God takes every variable into consideration before preparing the spiritual darkroom necessary for your purpose. Spiritual darkrooms help prepare us to move toward our destiny. However, the preparation for destiny is often not perceived as work that's related to purpose. As a result, believers become frustrated because the current environment does not look anything like their destiny or reflect the anointing on their life.

During the process in spiritual darkrooms, followers learn to depend on the Holy Spirit for strength and insight, and they find their source of faith through Jesus. Spiritual darkrooms are areas in which people seek to complete all the developmental stages while working toward their purpose. In the spiritual darkroom, followers are at risk for feeling lonely, even when they know they are not alone in the process because God is omnipresent. The loneliness often comes from being among others who have no insight as to your true identity or destiny—people who have a limited influence or power to assist in pushing you toward your purpose. In preparation for purpose, Jesus waits for anyone who is willing to believe that he is the author who controls the photographic chemicals that expose destinies. "But be ye doers of the word, and not hearers only, deceiving your own selves" (James 1:22 KJV). God waits for believers to understand the true meaning of the substance of their faith so he can empower them. He is greater than what he has made, including the process of reaching one's destiny. Therefore, rejoice and be glad in it.

Faith without works is dead. In preparation for the servants at the wedding in Cana, Mary's work was the necessary fuel to ignite the substance found only in faith. As she turned toward the servants and spoke with authority, a change from hopelessness to hopefulness took hold. Women were created to be life givers. Mary was created with the purpose to give life. She said yes to God, and as a result of her faith, Jesus was born. Because she was created to be a life giver and knew Jesus for who he is, she was able to facilitate Jesus's first miracle. Her previous experience of working with faith is what helped her to understand what was required to activate who Jesus is as the author and finisher of faith. Today, Jesus is waiting for people to speak life into things that appear to be roadblocks, deficits, or anything that keeps the rivers of living waters from enabling life to become more abundant. Jesus also can remove the roadblocks of life that hinder his workmanship. "For we are

His workmanship, created in Christ Jesus for good works, which God prepared beforehand, that we should walk in them" (Ephesians 2:10).

God called for Mary's work in the birthing process to activate who Jesus is in the natural. It was a most inopportune time for Mary to be pregnant, since she was promised to Joseph but not yet married. Jesus's hour to perform his first miracle was activated when Mary acted from a mindset that believed her master's word as a great source of power. This mindset gave her more insight into how to work with faith and the ability to see beyond Jesus as her son, but also as the son of God. "For God so loved the world that He gave His only begotten Son, that whoever believes in Him should not perish but have everlasting life" (John 3:16).

Faith not only attracts like a magnet, but it lives for work to come to it. In most elementary levels of education, a student is taught how magnets attract. The north pole of the magnet attracts the south pole of a second magnet, while the north pole of one magnet repels the other magnet's north pole. There is a common saying: "Like poles repel, unlike poles attract." So, can anything good come from a negative? God teaches his followers that by trusting the day of process or the steps that he has ordered, they will be able to rejoice and be glad in the day the Lord has made. The steps in the process are taken in a spiritual darkroom. Furthermore, everything concerning destiny is developed in a spiritual darkroom, where your purpose is revealed for you to live life and to live it more abundantly. Often the struggle found in the day the Lord has made or the steps he has ordered requires trusting him in the process he has designed. The steps he has ordered will bring you through; however, as followers, finding the balance between doubt, fear, and faith can be a struggle, but not impossible.

While I was at work the week before Christmas a few years ago, I had a very disturbing experience. It was about 10:00 p.m. when I remembered that I had left my gas stove turned on after preparing a cup of tea before I left for work earlier that afternoon. I was working the evening shift at the hospital and while making my rounds, I smelled something that reminded me of natural gas. Immediately, my mind went straight to my kitchen where I had turned on the gas stove before going upstairs to get dressed for work. I ran back to my unit in the hospital and explained to the other nurses that I had to leave. While driving home, so many thoughts filled with fears and doubts raced in my mind. What if my town house had burned down? What if the fire was so intense that it also burned down the homes connected to mine? All these what-ifs competed with the truth of who God is as my heavenly father, the purpose he placed inside me, and who I am to him. I thought about all the families in my neighborhood that could be homeless and the lives that might be lost in a fire. Then truth spoke: "Be anxious for nothing, but in everything by prayer and supplication, with thanksgiving, let your requests be made known to God; and the peace of God, which surpasses all understanding, will guard your hearts and minds through Christ Jesus" (Philippians 4:6–7). God's word provided me with instructions for coping with the struggle of my fears and doubts while believing that I Am will provide. It led me to trust him in the process of understanding that this is the day that the Lord has made, and I was able to rejoice and be glad in it. While I was driving home, I had to learn how to balance my fears, doubts, and my faith in who God is as I Am.

Doubts that people have during the process may be used in a dual purpose as they move toward destiny. God uses doubts as a tool in the spiritual dark places to further develop the measure of faith he has given. On the other hand, sometimes the adversary uses doubts to make a follower question God. "And we know that all things work together for good to those who love God, to those who are the called according to His purpose" (Romans 8:28). When I finally arrived home, the first thing I noticed was that the houses in my neighborhood were still standing. From where I parked my car, I could see the Christmas tree in my living room was untouched by fire. The white enamel gas stove was not scorched in spite of the flame and heat from the burner. While driving home, the only thing I wanted was for my neighbors to be safe. God's goodness and mercy followed me to work while the gas stove was left on and unattended. His goodness and mercy had continued while I was at the hospital providing patient care until I remembered that I had accidently left the gas stove on for several hours. I drove home with the purpose of turning the stove off and assessing any damage. "Surely goodness and mercy shall follow me all the days of my life; and I will dwell in the house of the LORD forever" (Psalm 23:6). Whatever type of day the Lord has made, God, in his goodness and mercy, is more than enough. His goodness and mercy enable people to see every day as a reason to rejoice and be glad despite the difficult circumstances that may appear in the steps he has ordered.

True worshippers can rejoice and be glad in the day the Lord has made because they know God as an unlimited source for every resource given to mankind. In spiritual darkrooms, true worshippers trust God in the areas that they cannot see their way through. Those who enter spiritual darkrooms do so trusting Jesus, through faith, as their new set of eyes illuminate a new way of understanding. Nevertheless, learning to balance doubts and fears while stepping out on faith is to be expected in the process.

Being glad and rejoicing would be the end result from the lessons learned in the process of trusting him while discovering one's true identity. Worth the struggle is a faith walk led by Jesus in a spiritual darkroom. Consequently, as Jesus is recognized as the author and finisher of their faith, true worshippers call on him by his many names that are often contrary to the circumstance facing them. To true worshippers, his name is I Am that gives a joyful noise to Elohim (the creator), El Elyon (the God most high), El Roi (the God who sees), El Shaddai (the all-sufficient one), Adonai (the Lord), Jehovah (the self-existent one), Jehovah-jireh (the Lord will provide), Jehovah-rapha (the Lord who heals), Jehovah-nissi (the Lord my banner), Jehovah-mekoddishkem (the Lord who sanctifies you), Jehovah-shalom (the Lord is peace), Jehovah-sabaoth (the Lord of hosts), Jehovah-raah (the Lord our shepherd), Jehovah-tisdkenu (the Lord our righteousness), and Jehovah-shammah (the Lord is there).

God will place believers in circumstances in which adversities and the adversary become tools used to strengthen people in the distance between rejoicing and being glad in the day the Lord has made.

Adversities may be used to distract believers from clearly seeing the path to true worship. When believers worship in truth and in spirit, every situation must bow to who God is and his piety. Because Jesus lives inside of people, everything outside of them must submit to who he is as the greater one over every adversity. Everything that God has given people to take possession over was given to them by faith; however, work is required to gain access to what God has already given them. "Now faith is the substance of things hoped for, the evidence of things not seen" (Hebrews 11:1). When God promises a thing to come to pass, faith becomes a part of the transaction process. Individuals will not be able to see naturally the thing that God has promised. However, faith will become their new way of thinking, and they will be able to see God in the midst of nothing, even in the absence of life.

> *Moses My servant is dead. Now therefore, arise, go over this Jordan, you and all this people, to the land which I am giving to them—the children of Israel. Every place that the sole of your foot will tread upon I have given you, as I said to Moses.*
>
> —Josh. 1:2–3

The distance between the land that God had provided for them as the children of Israel versus where they were in Jordan taught them to worship God in spirit and in truth. Learning to worship God in spirit and in truth became the distance from where they were in their walk with God to the Promised Land. Doubts and facts became their substance of belief of what God had promised rather than truth and faith in acquiring the Promised Land he gave them to possess. Although doubts and fears are often present in the pursuit, truth and faith must take control of the steering wheel when walking toward destiny. The distance between this is the day the Lord has made and let us rejoice and be glad in it is the faith to see true worship in spite of doubt. Having a mindset like Jesus empowers people to remove any misconceptions between the truth and facts. Every barrier, illness, death, feeling of hopelessness, fear, doubt, poverty, the adversary, unrighteousness, and other weapons formed against you must submit to the truth and not the facts. The battle with such adversities and the adversary is already won; however, the distance or gap between rejoicing and being glad in it is a faith fight that can only be done successfully by his spirit and in truth. When God gives a person something to possess, it will challenge their faith in believing that their only option is for God to get the glory. The challenge for some is their faith walk with God while acknowledging who he is and what he has already done. Sometimes, the faith walk can be a struggle and may get people dirty in the process, but it is worth the struggle because the battle is already won.

Believers are given the grace to know that the adversary has limited resources. Believers are connected to God through Jesus, who is the source that supplies all resources. So, it doesn't matter to a believer what type of day it is or the level of difficulty of circumstances in that day. Believers know who is in control and that even struggles have to submit to Jesus, which makes knowing him worth the struggle. God is Jehovah-jireh, a provider who gives believers the faith to rejoice and a state of being glad simply because they believe they are more than conquerors. Each day, believers must intentionally be aware of God's moves while learning how to work around the adversary and adversities. Living this way leads to rejoicing and being glad in the day the Lord has made within the process. Every move and every encounter toward adversities or the adversary must be led by his spirit. God instructs believers to rejoice and be glad in the day he has made; however, believers must have a mindset like Jesus, which is cultivated by faith. This act of believing is a conscious choice made by mature believers with an expectation that God is intentional in what he has prepared for his followers, regardless of the barriers.

"Therefore submit to God. Resist the devil and he will flee from you" (James 4:7). Only when believers find the kingdom of God and its righteousness does God reveal the power known as the Holy Spirit, who works from inside them. This power can also work to remove the adversary or adversities:

> *And I will pray the Father, and He will give you another Helper, that He may abide with you forever the Spirit of truth, whom the world cannot receive, because it neither sees Him nor knows Him; but you know Him, for He dwells with you and will be in you.*
>
> —John 14:16–17

God is a creator, and when he created man after his likeness and image, he also gave man the ability to solve challenges and overcome struggles. With the power of the Holy Spirit, God will use challenges to bring out hidden solutions inside his creations to resolve problems. God will use other people's challenges and or challenges found within you as a type of midwife to assist in birthing your purpose. There is nothing impossible for God to use or work with in bringing out the purpose that he has placed inside people. The one thing I have learned from having a learning disability is that it is never going away. However, as a result of living with the disability, I learned to pursue my purpose with tenacity. As I matured in the process, I noticed my tenacity growing even stronger in spite of my disability.

Fertilizer is recycled dead waste used to support life; it is used to promote growth, and adversities such as struggles are used to bring purpose to fruition in seeds of greatness. Look at the tares and the wheat and what it took for the two to grow together until it was time for harvest. The tares never disturbed the wheat's destiny or success. At the end of the day, the tares were used to prove how great God's faithfulness is. In the parable of the tares and the wheat, God is awesome in the way that he strategically instructs his followers on how to confront struggles and the adversary.

> *So the servants of the householder came and said unto him, Sir, didst not thou sow good seed in thy field? from whence then hath it tares? He said unto them, An enemy hath done this. The*

servants said unto him, Wilt thou then that we go and gather them up? But he said, Nay; lest while ye gather up the tares, ye root up also the wheat with them. Let both grow together until the harvest: and in the time of harvest I will say to the reapers, Gather ye together first the tares, and bind them in bundles to burn them: but gather the wheat into my barn.

—Matt. 13:27–30

The kingdom of God is much closer than most people can ever imagine. But the tares or weeds growing around the wheat make it difficult to see the plans and promises God has for the wheat. To many people, understanding how God's promises work while tares take root around God's wheat remains a mystery. God tells us in his word that he is omnipresent (i.e., always present) and omniscient (i.e., all-knowing). One might conclude, since God is omnipresent, that everything in the kingdom of God is also present. When we pray the Lord's prayer as followers in the faith, we are aligning our request on earth as it is in heaven. God has every intention for the supernatural concept of his kingdom to be more real to his followers than their perception of what is considered natural on earth. This may explain why this earth is not our home but only a place in time that followers travel through to get back to the place where they first knew God within the kingdom of heaven.

A couple of years ago, I gave my oldest son an example of how real and close the kingdom of God is in comparison to being in the natural world. "Tyrone," I said, "if the world saw me as a very wealthy person, what do you think would happen if we were out having dinner together in a restaurant and I accidentally left my money and credit cards at home?" My son responded, "I'm not sure." I told him that if I was a wealthy and well-known public icon, the manager of the restaurant would most likely offer me some type of credit based on society's perception of who I am and not on something that he could see or touch as a form of payment. Not having a wallet would have little bearing because my worth is in who I am. Who I am in God's eyes is worth more than having credit cards or money in my pocket and worth even more so as it relates to purpose.

Having access to the kingdom of God is more real than the access we have here on earth. As believers and heirs of God, there is a higher level of credibility when we come to know our identity or purpose.

This relationship between the believer and God is founded on who God is and not limited to being created in his image and likeness. Knowing who you are as heirs of God is more valuable than all the riches of the world. Most people are connected to other people by blood, by marriage, by association, or adoption; however, the connection is not validated until a relationship is formed. Our connection with God as our heavenly father is validated by having a personal relationship with Jesus. In this process of seeking a personal relationship with our heavenly father through Jesus, we find our purpose. It is in seeking a personal relationship with God that people discover and learn to live their identity. In the process of living one's purpose, life presents a more accurate version of the narrative that answers the question: Who am I? You will never find true joy until you let the real you come forth. What better way to rejoice in this day than knowing that the real you comes from the notion that God lives, moves, and has his being in you in spite of the daily challenges? This is no longer about salvation because believers have already been saved: It's about purpose—a time where the anointing meets the appointed time, and destiny has its day in court. People who have an intimate relationship with Jesus enter a transition period in the process where they grow from salvation to developing into their purpose. As a result of their personal relationship with Jesus, countless people in the Bible grew into their destiny. Making this transition took some work from each person in collaboration with faith to reach their purpose. They had to learn how to use what they had in their hands or how to work a room using faith in collaboration with their circumstances to pursue their destiny. "Working the room" is the ability to use faith in a situation in which essential tools to create a change in the natural are not available. Nevertheless, it is hope that pushes followers who believe that a change will take place in spite of any physical or natural evidence to the contrary. Another Mary, not Jesus's mother, had to learn to work the room. In this case, working the room is an understanding that works must collaborate with faith for the thing they hope for to be fruitful in a room of promise. At times, you will find yourself working a room among others who hate the idea that you were chosen to fulfill an assignment that only you can do. Some of those who are in the room watching you are waiting for you to fall flat on your face. Their jealousy takes on a form of pride because they put more significance on their own works. As a result, they do not collaborate their works with faith in the pursuit of destiny. Consider this anointing of Jesus:

> *And being in Bethany at the house of Simon the leper, as He sat at the table, a woman came having an alabaster flask of very costly oil of spikenard. Then she broke the flask and poured it on His head. But there were some who were indignant among themselves, and said, "Why was this fragrant oil wasted? For it might have been sold for more than three hundred denarii and given to the poor." And they criticized her sharply. But Jesus said, "Let her alone. Why do you trouble her? She has done a good work for Me. For you have the poor with you always, and whenever you wish you may do them good; but Me you do not have always. She has done what she could. She has come beforehand to anoint My body for burial. Assuredly, I say to you, wherever this gospel is preached in the whole world, what this woman has done will also be told as a memorial to her."*
>
> —Mark 14:3–9

The woman who anointed Jesus's feet with oil and Jesus's mother both knew how to work the room. Inherently, they saw something much deeper than what others were able to perceive by simply knowing the core of who Jesus is. Timing was everything. These women and other followers like them saw windows of opportunity by way of revelation and became game changers. They did not wake up that morning with the intent to change the world's view of who Jesus is as the son of God. Nevertheless, an unanticipated opportunity presented itself for these women where their anointing finally caught up with the appointed time. This was a day the Lord had made and their faith in who Jesus is became their reason to rejoice and be glad in it. Keep in mind that these women had to work the room first to get to the place where Jesus was revealed. In this place, rejoicing and being glad became a response to who God is rather than what he has done or what he was about to do. Working the room causes followers to be led by the Holy Spirit into a spiritual darkroom with the anticipation that God is going to reveal their destiny. This room is the place where purpose becomes further developed, and the desires of the believer's heart flows freely into identity. "But without faith it is impossible to please him: for he that cometh to God must believe that he is, and that he is a rewarder of them that diligently seek him" (Hebrews 11:6 KJV). A spiritual darkroom is entered by faith (Jesus), led by the Holy Spirit. The way to please God is to take faith (Jesus) by the hand into a spiritual darkroom. This is the day the Lord has made; let us rejoice and be glad in it is a faith-based prelude toward worshipping the Lord by declaring the end of a day before the beginning of that day. In this declaration, believers decree that no matter what happens during this day, God is omnipresent and omniscient. He is always in control of every day he makes. Worshipping God creates a joyful sound to the Lord. Calling out Jehovah-jireh is a sound captured by faith as it enters the presence of the Lord and proclaims, "I trust the power of your ability, that you are my provider."

In the parable of the tares and wheat, the servants were instructed by their master to adjust their mindset in how they saw the adversary. While having to work around the tares, it was the master's faith that empowered the servants to rejoice and become glad in the unexpected yet challenging circumstance with the tares. When believers begin consistently to hold a spiritual understanding of who God is when faced with adversities, then hope becomes the evidence of things not seen. Some believers are able to relate to the parable of the tares and wheat. They understand that in God, all things are possible because it's the day the Lord has made. Furthermore, the outcome of God's plan always turns out greater than its beginning. Spiritual darkrooms are not days that the Lord has made as a place to live in forever. They are designed as a place to support the development of the believer's purpose in preparation for the appointed time to live fully in their purpose. "Though your beginning was small, yet your latter end would increase abundantly" (Job 8:7). Many people, including believers, have questioned why the Lord would make a day in a spiritual darkroom filled with things that would lead people to doubt him, much less a room containing harmful things needed to live life with purpose. Nonetheless, God states in his word that we are "to rejoice and to be glad in it." These words can be problematic and perplexing for many people struggling with adversities. How can people rejoice and be glad when the day starts out very quickly filling up with sadness, hopelessness, sickness, incarceration, or a shortened life expectancy with no known cure? At times, we feel motherless or fatherless in dealing with major dysfunctions in the world, in our communities, among loved ones, and at our workplace. True worshippers are excited when they worship because in their spirit, they know the truth has the power to cause something wonderful to be exposed.

I remember that as a teenager, I would find myself lying in bed at night unable to sleep. Feelings of uncertainty about who I was kept me from resting peacefully. When these feelings came to mind, I would look out my window and search the stars hoping to find my purpose in this place called life. At the same time, I was praying to God. I asked him who I was and what was my purpose on earth. God's response was for me to find the way through process and by trusting the one who made the process. In other words, "seek first the kingdom of God and His righteousness" (Matthew 6:33). God revealed that I needed to trust the journey or process if I wanted to know my purpose.

> *For I know the thoughts that I think toward you, says the LORD, thoughts of peace and not of evil, to give you a future and a hope. Then you will call upon Me and go and pray to Me, and I will listen to you. And you will seek Me and find Me, when you search for Me with all your heart.*
>
> —Jer. 29:11–13

For some believers, the struggle to better understand who created the day of process takes place daily. The revelation of who God is becomes the breaking point and the breakthrough that places people into a state of mind of rejoicing and being glad despite the type of day they are having. As I reflect as a much older woman, I can see God's footprints and his handprints in the worst days of my life from childhood to adulthood. However, because I had to learn to trust the journey, I know now that God does his best work in what appears to be a mess. In these places and moments, the Holy Spirit gets very excited, and the truth of who God is, is revealed. He gets the glory.

As a teenager who did not know my purpose spiritually, I was not aware that I was in a spiritual darkroom while I lay awake at night with feelings of uncertainty. God was prepping me for my destiny, and the process required a personal, intimate relationship with him through Jesus, managed by the Holy Spirit. God was not ignoring me by not answering my questions. But, like a potter, he worked the answers into the process of allowing me to trust the one who created the process. Answers to questions asked during the process sometimes are revealed after we demonstrate faithfulness in the one who created the journey. When we don't take time to understand the importance of the process, too much focus is placed on challenges met along the way and not on the promises to reveal our identity. Faith is a required substance in the day of process that the Lord has made. Promises and guarantees are attached to each day simply because God gave his word, and his word is faith through Jesus.

Imagine having a famous fashion designer create a custom article of clothing for you. Just knowing and appreciating the workmanship that goes into creating a designer original speaks volumes. With the designer's name on the label, the piece of clothing could well continue to increase in value. This concept is the same expectation that God looks for in people who will acknowledge him as creator. As people work the process, their trust in who God is deepens, and they spend less time and energy feeling anxious about the uncertainties or hardships simply because the value is not in the item itself, but in the one who created the item. I often caught myself placing too much importance on my discomfort level when attempting to overcome challenges. I realize now that my focus needs to be on the strengths I have as I overcome challenges, rather than perceiving my stress level as something bigger than the challenge itself. I have learned in the process of rejoicing and being glad in the day the Lord has made to respond to the challenges instead of reacting to the stress they impose. As a student with dyslexia, I was forced to learn how to cope effectively with my learning disability. Over the years, I have failed a test, class, or subject; I even failed the nursing program twice—at two different schools. I spent several thousands of dollars for my failed attempts in school and registered nursing programs. However, in every case where I have failed, I got up and tried again. My disappointments, hurt, and embarrassment were not enough to keep me down because my hope was not placed on the things that led to my failures. My hope was fed by my heart's desire and my vision of becoming a registered nurse. Hope and desire pushed me constantly to overcome failures that I could clearly see and was often reminded of.

In Matthew 15:35–38, the author shares that Jesus fed over 4,000 men plus women and children with seven loaves and a few fish. Left over from this meal were seven large baskets of bread and fish. In Matthew 14:19–21, we are told that Jesus fed 5,000 men plus women and children with five loaves of bread and just two fish. Afterward, 12 baskets of leftovers remained. David who fought Goliath had five stones, but it took only one stone to defeat the giant. God will use a single person, place, or thing as a conduit to do great things through you and for his glory. However, faith in God must be accessible to be activated. The baskets of food scraps left over from feeding thousands of hungry people could have been a reminder or a testimony to Jesus's disciples to prevent them from losing sight of their source of faith (Jesus). In John 15:5, Jesus informs people that he is the vine and we are the branches. If we stay joined to him and allow him to stay joined to us, then we shall come to fruition. Without Jesus, followers cannot be effectively productive in their purpose. God will use what we have left, such as our last dime, to demonstrate that all things are possible if we only believe and are plugged into him. The height of the miracle was not in the feeding of the 5,000 or the 4,000. It was the leftovers. At times, what God has done for you will encourage others to place their trust in him. When you look back at what God has done in your life, the things that remind you of his greatness make you appreciate who God is. The memory becomes the object of worship and compels you to praise him. If you wind up in a tight place, find your deliverance in your past experiences with God.

> *You are our epistle written in our hearts, known and read by all men; clearly you are an epistle of Christ, ministered by us, written not with ink but by the Spirit of the living God, not on tablets of stone but on tablets of flesh, that is, of the heart.*
>
> —2 Cor. 3:2–3

Testimonies come from our inner voice empowered by the lessons we learned along the way in the process of living our purpose. Sometimes, they are like the 12 baskets of food scraps left over. God sees people as a type of epistle, a living letter from one who has a voice to share valuable lessons with others about the struggle one encounters in discovering and living one's purpose. This voice can be used as validation and evidence of God's possibilities in the hope of encouraging others that the struggle is worth it. As followers, we are taught to walk by faith and not by sight. Needless to say, the 12 baskets of food scraps were not only used as a symbol of faith in what God has done, but in what he is able to do, and exceedingly more! The power of your testimony is what is left; that is, the lessons learned in the struggle during the process of living one's purpose further develop a person's fellowship with Christ. Do not allow your perception of what you have remaining to distract you from what God can do with what you have left. What you have left from the last battle of faith is what empowers you to fight the next battle of faith.

A person's relationship with God, which is often expressed through worship, is evidence of the increasing value in knowing the one who made the day. Speaking of God, Lamentations 3:23 declares, "Great is Your faithfulness." Jesus is not only the author and finisher of our faith, but God is faithful to his word and to the faith of the follower who believes in him as the word. Too often, believers ask for more faith rather than just believing in who Jesus is. Understanding the substance of who Jesus is as our source of faith will transform our perception in any situation that needs change. Every adversity and the adversary must submit to God; this is the reason that some believers choose to rejoice knowing the struggle was worth it. People who find it difficult to rejoice and be glad in the day the Lord has made can find life very challenging until they receive a revelation of who God is in the challenge. This type of mindset can be achieved through the process of seeking first the kingdom of God and his righteousness. The kingdom of God is a place that can be found within people by way of seeking. "But seek ye first the kingdom of God, and his righteousness; and all these things shall be added unto you" (Matthew 6:33 KJV). The keys that God has for people who seek him give total access. Just as Jesus is the truth and the way, God is the process in discovering our true identity and purpose. Through the experiences along the process, followers learn how to trust in the one who created the process. Lessons learned become a lifestyle that proclaims, "I will trust God's word in the process simply because he is in control." In the day the Lord has made, preparation develops a believer's purpose.

As an example, think of a cast-iron pan for cooking. Cast iron can become very hot in the oven and not burn. Followers going through the process also will not burn when under extreme heat and fire. The cast-iron pan can be described as heavy with a hard surface. For some believers, the waiting period for the appointed time can be a heavy and hard journey to face. The substance prepared in a cast-iron pan is like the substance found in believers, poured into a pan for molding and shaping for the sake of purpose and their true identity. In this process, believers are prepared by the things they have learned along the way between their anointing time and their appointed time. This is the place in the process where something good comes out of a negative, and rejoicing and being glad in the day the Lord has made becomes a natural and spiritual response. There is one road that people can take in understanding the process, and it begins with renewing one's thought process to be like Christ Jesus. "'For My thoughts are not your thoughts, nor are your ways My ways,' says the LORD" (Isaiah 55:8).

I have had the pleasure and opportunity to facilitate both reflection groups and relaxation groups at my place of work. As a psychiatric nurse to an inpatient population, I would often share with them the benefits that come when people change the way they think. Taking on a new perception or thought process would lead them into making better choices. As a leader for both groups, I would start by explaining the need for a healthier thought process. Our bodies, behaviors, and attitudes follow our thought process, which determines our reactions when making choices. Changing the thought process worked effectively with several of my patients. However, looking at this same concept as a person in pursuit of understanding the day of process means considering how Jesus thinks, which provides me with a better idea of when I should be rejoicing and being glad in it.

> *Let this mind be in you which was also in Christ Jesus, who, being in the form of God, did not consider it robbery to be equal with God, but made Himself of no reputation, taking the form of a bondservant, and coming in the likeness of men. And being found in appearance as a man, He humbled Himself and became obedient to the point of death, even the death of the cross.*
>
> —Phil. 2:5–8

"For we walk by faith, not by sight" (2 Corinthians 5:7). "For in him we live and move and have our being" (Acts 17:28). While people are being prepared in the spiritual darkroom as it relates to purpose, God sees every negative already in pictured form, custom framed by his word, and signed by the blood of Jesus as a finished work in every individual. Can any good thing come from a negative? The answer is yes. "And we know that all things work together for good to those who love God, to those who are the called according to His purpose" (Romans 8:28).

I had a dream several years ago that I was taking a walk in a new dimension that I had never experienced before with my natural eyes. During my walk, I saw some pennies on the ground, and as I walked away from the pennies, I saw more valuable coins—nickels, dimes, and quarters. Then, I started picking up the coins. I heard a voice, and I knew in my heart it was God. He asked, "What are you doing?" I told him that I had found some coins on the ground and no one was around to claim them, so I was picking them up. I explained that I thought I would be justified in keeping the coins I found. God responded by saying, "You are right, and you are wrong in your thinking process. The pennies you walked past were there for you as well as the silver coins you collected and kept. The way you think about pennies or what appears to be small or insignificant to you and others makes you feel justified with your self-righteousness to walk by them. Apparently, pennies are not important enough for you to humble yourself in public because of their apparent value." God continued, "I was the one who allowed the coins including the pennies you saw to be there for you to collect and have. But because of your foolish pride, you could not see that it was the pennies and not the silver that have the greatest value. The purpose of the pennies was to place you in a position to be humble." From that dream, I learned the true value of a penny and how God teaches me humility by reaching down to pick up pennies even if others feel that a penny is of little or no value. Whenever I see a penny on the ground and if it appears no one is claiming it, I will pick it up because I know the value of this coin and how God will use it to keep me humble to him and his plan for my purpose. I came to realize that God is using the value of a penny to teach me how to develop an awareness of serving people around me who may appear to be less valuable or insignificant. Just the other day, my newlywed husband and I were waiting through a nine-hour delay at the Miami airport as we were returning home from a vacation in the Dominican Republic. During our stay in the Dominican, I saw no pennies on the ground, but as I reached the gate for our departure from Miami to Richmond, VA, I found a penny lying on the ground close to where my husband and I were sitting. When

I picked up the penny, I knew that God was planning to use me in a significant way in serving him and for his glory. It takes faith for me to pick up a penny knowing that people could be watching and thinking, "Seriously?" This time in my heart, I knew God was intentional about preparing my mind and heart to help someone who appeared to be insignificant, but in God's eyes; they were power moves in his plans. However, I did not know when or how all of this was going to work out, but I believed that God was up to something. In the course of waiting and having to deal with this unexpected delay, I saw people in need of a hand. I befriended a young mother traveling with her four-year-old daughter who was sound asleep in her lap for several hours right across from where I was sitting. She asked me if I could hold her daughter so she could use the bathroom. She transferred her daughter into my arms for me to hold and comfort. The child opened her eyes for a few minutes and saw me, but she did not try to leave nor cry out for her mother in fear or distress. When her mother returned, I offered to get them some food using the food vouchers that were given to us by the airline. When I left to get the food, I saw a young woman sitting alone a few gates away from us. It was 3:00 a.m., and she seemed to be trying to keep warm and find a way to rest while waiting for her flight. I tapped her on the shoulder and told her where she could get blankets and pillows that the airline had provided. I could tell by the way she reacted that she spoke and understood very little English, which led me to believe that she may not have completely understood what I was saying. On my way back to my gate, I noticed that she still looked like she was struggling to stay warm and comfortable. After I brought food back for my husband and the young mother and her daughter, I grabbed some extra pillows and a blanket and walked back to find the young woman waiting for her flight. I found her and gave her the pillows and a blanket; she received them with a warm smile and said thank you.

I recall all this to show how God does significant, big things through small gestures of kindness through people who are willing to humble themselves in spite of what others may say or do. God is so big on small things that he uses seeds in his word to illustrate great things as a by-product of faith: "If you have faith as a mustard seed, you will say to this mountain, 'Move from here to there,' and it will move; and nothing will be impossible for you" (Matthew 17:20). Having a mindset like Jesus empowers individuals to see the value in things that others view as less valuable. God used pennies to teach and remind me to be humble, so when I become rich in silver and gold, my mentality toward people, places, and things will be like the mind of a servant who is after the things that reflect God's heart.

YOUR ADVERSARY IS YOUR SPARRING
PARTNER

CHAPTER 4

In 2016, my ex-husband Jerry was diagnosed with ALS also known as Lou Gehrig's disease or motor neuron disease. ALS is a progressive neurological disease that causes the neurons that control voluntary muscles (motor neurons) to degenerate, according to the National Institutes of Health. In October 2016, at age 63, he was given 18 months to live.

As the mother to our young adult child and two teenage children and as a registered nurse, I decided with Jerry that he would move into my home and that I would become his primary caregiver. With the support of our children, his brothers, sister, sister-in-law, and the hospice community, we were at his side. His physiological, spiritual, and mental health-care needs as well as bereavement support were provided to guide him in this journey. Unfortunately, Jerry's way of coping with this disease and the bereavement process often involved confrontations with me regarding his personal anger with God. Every day he opened his eyes, it was a reminder of the effects of the disease and what he could never have again, which became increasingly devastating and depressing to him. I chose to use acts of kindness in response to his anger and turned the other cheek. I often allowed myself to take the brunt of his anger simply because I was the closest thing to God he had around to kick and curse. His abuse toward me did not change despite the support I gave.

I originally thought that God wanted me to write about Jerry's reaction to his condition, treatment, and prognosis. But God revealed to me, "No! I want you to share with others the process in moving from this is day the Lord has made to let us rejoice and be glad in it and realizing that the process in trusting God's word is worth the struggle while coping with life's challenges." This same concept can be applied to discovering and living one's destiny. God gives people the strength, grace, and mercy needed to go through the process and not try to go around it or avoid it all together. "Your sandals shall be iron and bronze; as your days, so shall your strength be" (Deuteronomy 33:25–26). This is the day the Lord has made is a voice from God providing a sense of security for people reaching their destiny. It is this same mindset that helps people with the process of understanding: "The steps of a good man are ordered by the LORD, and He delights in his way" (Psalm 37:23).

God looks for people who are willing to see him as far greater than any death sentence, disease, adversity, or challenge that seems too big to be handled single-handedly or by a community. How does one rejoice and be glad when the day made by God is filled with problems and the only place available to work out these challenges is in a spiritual darkroom? The answer lies in knowing and trusting in the one who created this day in spite of its problems. People are created in the likeness of God and in his image; therefore, they are given the power to be creative. Some days made by God are filled with challenges, problems, adversities, and unanswered questions instead of being filled with good times, good health, and answers for every problem. However, God the creator has placed solutions to these difficult times in the minds and the hearts of people. Believers in a collaboration of work and faith go through a process of discovering and living life with purpose. This process helps uncover the solution hidden inside believers, which will change how they see themselves and how the world sees God.

While believers are in training for purpose, God will assign sparring partners to prepare them for their appointed time. Just imagine the day the Lord has made is a date with a sparring partner to further develop your purpose from within. God expects believers to rejoice and be glad in the day knowing that the preparation process is for their purpose. Doing so comes by faith. Believers know who their creator is, and because God stands by his word, his word is a force to be reckoned with.

I used to look at my place of employment as an environment in which to promote a nursing career within the federal government. I soon became discouraged and saw my workplace as a job, but God revealed to me that what I perceived as a job, he was using for something much greater. Once my eyes were open to what God was doing, I looked at my job as a workout gym where God was permitting me to develop a set of special skills that would empower me to fulfill my purpose. These exercises allow followers to work on their callings and gifts; toning up these presents from God results in pain that must be endured to bring forth the gifts. Sometimes, pain is used as a sign to inform patients and those in the health field of the healing process. When pain is viewed as part of the healing process, it becomes a necessary component in getting something much better than what you had before.

God informs his followers that the workout is not theirs, but the Lord's, who strengthens believers by his might to rejoice and to be glad in it. The day of process is not a battle for people to fight but a period of transformation or getting in shape to discover purpose. "Thus says the LORD to you: 'Do not be afraid nor dismayed because of this great multitude, for the battle is not yours, but God's'" (2 Chronicles 20:15).

In this battle, there's a difference between sparring and fighting. Fighting is all about stealing, killing, or the adversary's attempt to destroy you, whereas sparring perfects your gifts for your purpose. If more believers could perceive adversity as though it was sent by God to be a sparring partner, they would have perfect peace rather than increased levels of anxiety. This perception would allow believers to know that the discomfort we face from adversities can bring out our hidden talents. In addition, it would encourage believers to rejoice and be glad rather than feel defeated by the enemy. The sparring partner objective is not to teach the believer how to fight between good and evil; it is a workout of removing layers of things that do not foster the discovery of their true identity and living life with purpose. In rope-a-dope, one fighter covers up and often leans back against the ropes to allow the opponent to become exhausted by throwing punches. A tired opponent cannot effectively defend himself late in the fight and can more easily be defeated. Rope-a-dope is an effective coping strategy to push out your purpose when you face an adversary.

Faith is the substance of things hoped for and the evidence of things not seen. Faith without works is dead. Works is another word for hope. It is impossible to foster faith or to walk in faith without hope. Faith is the root that supports the existence of life, whereas hope is the resurrection in turning dead things to life. Jesus is the resurrection and the life, and he is faith and faithful: "He who believes in me, as the scripture has said, out of his heart will flow rivers of living water" (John 7:38–39). God never promised the day he has made to be free from adversity. In fact, some days the struggle appears more intense than ever. Consequently, he did promise followers who are walking through the valley of the shadow of death that his rod and staff would comfort them and that no weapons formed against them would prosper. Believers are given a place of rest simply by knowing who Jesus is. "For the gifts and the calling of God are irrevocable" (Romans 11:29). Each day the Lord has made is a gift to discover the callings from God and an opportunity to serve God in your purpose. He only supplies our daily bread, but he is the God of not enough who can turn it into more than enough. This is a good reason for believers to rejoice and be glad in it. For God said it, leaving no cause why he should take it away. As a result, believers are empowered to experience rejoicing and being glad during moments of trouble through worship.

But the hour cometh, and now is, when the true worshippers shall worship the Father in spirit and in truth: for the Father seeketh such to worship him. God is a Spirit: and they that worship him must worship him in spirit and in truth.

—John 4:23–24 KJV

"Then the LORD answered me and said: 'Write the vision and make it plain on tablets, that he may run who reads it. For the vision is yet for an appointed time; but at the end it will speak, and it will not lie. Though it tarries, wait for it; because it will surely come, it will not tarry.'"

—Hab. 2:2–4

The just shall live by his faith. When the vision appears unclear, wait for it. In periods of weakness in the day the Lord has made, believers are made strong in between rejoicing and being glad in it.

Strategies are often used to win in the boxing ring as well as in spiritual warfare. In boxing, rope-a-dope is a strategy to appear weak and persuade an opponent to attack and fall into a trap. A rope-a-dope strategy can tire out an adversary while you plan for victory.

We also glory in tribulations, knowing that tribulation produces perseverance; and perseverance, character; and character, hope. Now hope does not disappoint, because the love of God has been poured out in our hearts by the Holy Spirit who was given to us.

—Rom. 5:3–5

Don't allow the things you can see with your eyes or the thoughts influenced by carnality to distract you or dilute what God has faithfully given to you. How can you cope with stressors and the expectation of receiving punches from the adversities of life?

Countless expectant women use the Lamaze method during labor and delivery. This method of childbirth involves exercises and breathing control to assist with pain relief with or without medication. Lamaze helps women experiencing painful contractions. Labor pains help expectant woman to know when to push. The Lamaze strategy helps the mother stay focused on the birthing process and not become quickly exhausted by fighting against or reacting to the labor pains. Women must work in the process of giving birth to a baby. This same concept can be used in understanding the connection between work and faith.

> *What does it profit, my brethren, if someone says he has faith but does not have works? Can faith save him? If a brother or sister is naked and destitute of daily food, and one of you says to them, "Depart in peace, be warmed and filled," but you do not give them the things which are needed for the body, what does it profit? Thus, also faith by itself, if it does not have works, is dead.*
>
> —James 2:14–20

Labor pains during contractions signal women that work must collaborate with faith to deliver their baby. Any type of labor pain is uncomfortable, yet it is necessary to bring forth fruit. The work becomes a requirement in that season of discomfort. However, pushing toward purpose becomes much greater than the season of discomfort. Even if there is no evidence of the crown of the baby's head, the woman must keep pushing with each contraction unless it becomes harmful or ineffective toward purpose. In the labor pains of life's adversities, God looks for people to worship him. True worshippers know labor pains of life are a sign that the promise is coming. That prospect outweighs the discomforts suffered in the process. In times of weakness, true worshippers lift the name of God on high because they know that God has a plan that incorporates the power from the Holy Spirit as the only source for strength. Faith is required to support our purpose until fruition arrives. While working toward it, labor must collaborate with faith, for without work, faith is dead.

> *For indeed the gospel was preached to us as well as to them; but the word which they heard did not profit them, not being mixed with faith in those who heard it. For we who have believed do enter that rest.*
>
> —Heb. 4:2–3

The place of rest in the process comes from believing that each step has been ordered by God to bring them to their destiny. Simply resting in what he has said he would do is an act of faith. However, this requires a mindset like Jesus in understanding the importance of being transformed by the renewing of one's mind. "Seek ye first the kingdom of God . . . all these things shall be added" (Matthew 6:33 KJV). "Let this mind be in you, which was also in Christ Jesus" (Philippians 2:5). Both verses offer followers more bang for their buck as it relates to the process of discovering one's purpose and arriving at the resting place where one can rejoice and be glad in the day the Lord has made.

Taking on the way Jesus thinks empowers followers to change their behavior because the way they think will direct the way they choose to act. In general, how people think like Christ before the transformation is often based on instinct and what they perceive as self-righteousness. Men who have an instinct to choose knowledge or self-righteousness will never have the wisdom of God, who is omnipresent, omniscient, and truth. Thank God, he chose to love the world first, rather than waiting for the world to choose to love him first. Finding the kingdom of God and its righteousness means following God's thought process, his ways, and his plans. In the process of finding him, moreover, you will discover your purpose. The kingdom of God becomes revealing through having a personal relationship with God through Jesus. Religion simply points in the direction of finding God but cannot reveal who he is. The process of transforming into having a mindset like Jesus prepares people to know who God is as they seek him in spite of the struggle.

In this process, God remakes people like a potter who transforms his clay into works of art with unique functions. Faith is the mindset necessary in seeking first the kingdom of God and its righteousness, especially going through the challenges of being made over again in the potter's hands. When followers choose to go through the process of discovering the kingdom of God, faith is better developed, and tenacity becomes a character-building trait in discovering their true identity in the kingdom. "For in Him we live, and move, and have our being" (Acts 17:28). As believers if we live, move, and have our being in God, we are empowered to live and function in our destinies. So, why become anxious about the distance between this is the day the Lord has made and reaching the place where one is rejoicing and being glad in it? The believer's purpose is a book that Jesus already wrote and published before he created the day. Because of this, he instructs believers to rejoice and be glad in it.

I remember as a teenager learning how to cook from watching my mother. But when I started to cook, I experienced failure after failure. Luckily, my tenacity grew right alongside my failed attempts, and further experience taught me how to perfect my cooking. Those failed attempts helped me learn. Every day the Lord has made to the point of rejoicing and being glad in it works out to be a good thing. "And we know that all things work together for good to them that love God, to them who are the called according to his purpose" (Romans 8:28).

When I finally learned how to do things in life such as cooking, being a parent, and completing nursing school, I succeeded through many failed attempts. I understand now that the disappointments from my flop dishes kept me going back to the kitchen to try again. My getting kicked out of the nursing program because of failing grades encouraged me to keep pressing to become a registered nurse. I had to find another nursing program in another school that accepted me, just so I could try again and again. I finally became a registered nurse, and in six years, I graduated with a Doctor of Nursing Practice degree despite my learning disability. God doesn't intend for people to stay in a state of what appears to be failure for long—just long enough for them to see his glory in using challenges and failures as a tool to create success stories in the lives of ordinary people. Although the search for who Jesus is can be a struggle, it is in that struggle where the blessing of who he is becomes strength to the weak.

> *Therefore being justified by faith, we have peace with God through our Lord Jesus Christ: By whom also we have access by faith into this grace wherein we stand, and rejoice in hope of the glory of God. And not only so, but we glory in tribulations*

also: knowing that tribulation worketh patience; and patience, experience; and experience, hope: And hope maketh not ashamed; because the love of God is shed abroad in our hearts by the Holy Ghost which is given unto us.

—Rom. 5:1–5

The substance of who Jesus is empowers and brings followers to the place of rejoicing and being glad because everything needed in living life with purpose is found in the substance of who Jesus is. This is one of the main reasons that God commands his followers to seek first the kingdom of God and his righteousness and promises that "these things shall be added unto you" (Matthew 6:33). The kingdom contains the substance of who God is and the destiny of those who seek who he is. God may not take away the challenges in the day the Lord has made; however, his instructions for followers to rejoice and be glad in it require an act of faith. Faith requires a mindset that views God as being greater than anything or anyone that appears to be a threat or a barrier to destiny. For example, he never changed the color of my skin every time I was discriminated against, and he never cured me from dyslexia. But because of his grace and mercy, he taught me that despite these things he has given me a level of success so that others will know it was him who brought me to succeed and not me or another individual. God's great faithfulness illuminates in seasons of struggles. His faithfulness forever sees our destiny and not our past.

For the weapons of our warfare are not carnal, but mighty through God to the pulling down of strongholds. Casting down imaginations, and every high thing that exalteth itself against the knowledge of God, and bringing into captivity every thought to the obedience of Christ.

—2 Cor. 10:4–5

The weapons used for warfare are not carnal or based on emotions alone, such as hatred, doubt, betrayal, nastiness, jealousy, or envy.

Weapons such as worship can be obtained from knowing who he is. Believers become more empowered in the struggle when they realize that through tribulation comes patience and that patience helps them understand and respond to the things they have experienced. In the end, hope becomes the final outcome.

THE WEIGHT AND REST IN KNOWING GOD IN THE STRUGGLE

CHAPTER 5

As Jerry's last primary caregiver, I learned for myself about the rest and weight in knowing God. I physically and spiritually carried Jerry throughout the last two years of his journey with ALS. I also had to learn how and when to balance the resting phase along with the work phase. In each phase of the dying process, Jerry became more dependent on me and other family members. My rest from working with Jerry was believing in and trusting God's word and the value of knowing God's presence in moments when all hell was breaking loose in the disease process. Near the end, I called the family in Virginia, North Carolina, South Carolina, and New York to let them know that Jerry might have only 72 hours to live. I recall the last 24 hours of Jerry's life when he became even more dependent on me. I took that weekend off from work and with 24 hours of planning and preparing, I cooked a feast for friends and family to celebrate what God had done and what he was about to do in Jerry's journey.

On March 17, 2019, I heard Jerry calling out for help every two hours on the two-way monitor system kept in my bedroom and in his room. I had a house full of family members to share Jerry's last few days on earth, and no one could hear his cry for help but me. Each time he called out, he wanted to go to the bathroom or to voice his discomfort. This was the first time I had ever observed Jerry being so restless and afraid. I found rest in confronting Jerry that he was in transition from earth to heaven, and I promised him that he would not go through this transition alone. I reassured him that it was a part of my calling to provide him with the reassurance necessary to have a smooth transition to a spiritual world where the disease process would end. I found my rest in knowing that Jerry would soon be in the presence of the Lord and that he would finally have a perfect peace, which the world could neither give nor explain. Although I bore the weight of holding him up and assisting him to the bathroom with an impaired gait, I still had to find the rest in God's promises to help me balance the weight and the rest. Assisting Jerry to the bathroom was like carrying dead weight. There came a moment where his weight was too heavy for me to bear by myself. I woke up one of my adult daughters for assistance in transferring him back to bed. Later that same afternoon, his family from North Carolina and South Carolina arrived. During this weekend, the family enjoyed fellowship during dinner, and we sat alongside Jerry's bed to share with him words of encouragement and our love for him. Although I got only one and a half hours of sleep that night, I found rest in God's grace to cook and serve dinner and gave each family a homemade sweet potato pie to take home. Rest for me was celebrating who God was throughout the ALS disease process and seeing and assisting in Jerry's pain and suffering while going through it. This book came out of Jerry's journey and the work and learning how to rest in who God is by seeking his presence in the day-of process. I realize that walking alongside Jerry in his three-year journey of coping with ALS became a faith walk of learning to trust God in spite of difficult circumstances. I learned to worship God in adversities and taught Jerry in his last few days on earth to worship God in his pain, discomfort, anger, depression, and fear of the unknown.

The Saturday of our family weekend and the day before he passed away, our children, grandchildren, my brother Anthony, Jerry, and I held hands in a circle in the living room. We began to worship God.

We did not ask God for anything but thanked him for everything. We called out everything we know he is. That Saturday was the last day Jerry got out of bed and sat in the living room among his family. In spite of his rapid decline in health, I found rest in baking sweet potato pies and cooking dinner for family members who came to visit. With little sleep, strangely enough I found rest walking up a mountain by trusting God with the limitations of what I had in my hand in making life more comfortable for Jerry. What I had in my hand was knowledge about how to make others feel comfortable from my nursing experience, education, and knowledge of how to work a kitchen. God had used my training in how to cook to reshape and mold me into purpose by teaching me to appreciate process. God used the kitchen to perfect my cooking while teaching me the this-is-the-day-of process. I knew I was extremely limited in changing Jerry's outcome. Nevertheless, my source of strength was getting to know God as a friend in the kitchen and how his grace would be sufficient. To rest is to know and see who God is in every situation while surrendering to him as the great I Am. One of the most amazing things about Jesus is that he is not only faith, but he is so faithful. Consequently, quite often he is more faithful in believing and trusting the process than are people who go through it. He also remains steadfast in the promises he has spoken over their lives.

Years ago, when I was at my worst in learning how to cook, he still believed that I would become a very good cook simply because he believed and trusted the process. God trusted in me while I was yet struggling to believe in what he promised and said he was going to do. Yet he found rest in his word while I was at my worst. God is still waiting for so many people to find rest in who he is when faced with challenges in the process. "He said to his servants, 'Stay here with the donkey while I and the boy go over there. We will worship and then we will come back to you'" (Genesis 22:5 NIV). Abraham and Isaac left the others behind and worshipped the Lord in truth and in spirit. When Abraham took his son and left without the servants, he carried the weight of not knowing that there would be a ram caught in a bush as a burnt offering. Like a true worshipper, his response to their situation was believing God is Jehovah-jireh. His faith was never based on the fact that a ram stuck in a bush was waiting for them; rather, it was based on his ability to trust God as a provider.

The weight that Abraham carried became the substance of who God is to him and the core of his strength. The weight that he carried represented the value of Abraham's purpose and calling as the father of faith and a friend of God. The weight that is carried can often be determined by the type of personal relationship one has with God. Abraham's rest was knowing he was a personal friend of God. There is a weight when walking with God as a friend; nevertheless, there is also a rest in knowing who God is in the day that the Lord has made. The concept of weight used in this example is not used as something negative but as a type of responsibility required from others who have a desire in developing their faith in their walk with God. Faith like a muscle does not multiply but enlarges as it is developed through having one's faith tested by the weight of struggles. The measure of faith Abraham was given became the glue in their friendship regardless of the day-to-day struggles he faced.

> *But he who did not know, yet committed things deserving of stripes, shall be beaten with few. For everyone to whom much is given, from him much will be required; and to whom much has been committed, of him they will ask the more.*
>
> —Luke 12:48

True worshippers have developed spiritual muscles through weight training. These muscles have equipped them to rejoice and be glad knowing that the struggle was worth it. What brings true worshippers to a place of rest is knowing that living their purpose makes the struggle with weight training worth it. The weight of developing one's faith is encountering successfully all the lessons in preparation for purpose in spite of the struggle of not being able to see whether there has been any measurable sign of progress. The weight prepares and develops individuals to succeed and not have the responsibilities of success become overwhelming. Furthermore, the weight God gives also provides a balance to prevent people from tripping. Believers deeply appreciate Jesus waiting for them to build up their strength to carry the weight that he has placed on them as they live life with purpose and more abundantly. The distance or gap in the day-of process between this is the day the Lord has made and let us rejoice and be glad in it is the understanding of the balance between rest and working out in the weight room. Jesus is waiting for us to bulk up in faith to carry the weight or the responsibilities that come with the success that purpose carries. He rests with patience because he knows the required weight of faith necessary for destiny to become effective in its purpose.

> *And on the seventh day God ended His work which He had done, and He rested on the seventh day from all His work which He had done. Then God blessed the seventh day and sanctified it, because in it He rested from all His work which God had created and made.*
>
> —Gen. 2:2–3

There is an art and a science in weight training; however, some people do not understand the importance that rest plays. The resting phase allows muscles to heal, regroup, and recover after the workout. As it relates to the process in the day the Lord has made, once individuals have applied the work needed, God allows them to rest in the faith that he is in control of every outcome. This resting phase is just as important as the resting phase in bodybuilding. If the measure of faith that God gives to people can be viewed as muscles for bodybuilding, development of faith can be seen as a place of rest from a previous workout. A resting phase is required to successfully increase faith and more deeply understand the glory of God and the substance of who Jesus is (faith).

> *Come to Me, all you who labor and are heavy laden, and I will give you rest. Take My yoke upon you and learn from Me, for I am gentle and lowly in heart, and you will find rest for your souls. For My yoke is easy and My burden is light.*
>
> —Matt. 11:28–30

The ability to find rest after work while still facing adversity is to know Jesus is omnipresent. He is present while you are working as well as resting, when he often finds himself waiting for you to show up just so he can show out. The resting phase in the process of this is the day the Lord has made encourages people to sit away from the workroom in the promises of God. In addition, rest gives faith the space it needs to do what God said he will do after your workout. "There remains therefore a rest for the people of God. For he who has entered His rest has himself also ceased from his works as God did from His" (Hebrews 4:9–10).

As people continue to work on one particular muscle without rest, they are at risk for injuring that overworked muscle. Too often, people work more than what is required in partnership with faith. As a result, they place themselves at risk of becoming frustrated and injured because they don't know when to stop working and when to begin the resting phase by knowing who God is.

> And a great windstorm arose, and the waves beat into the boat, so that it was already filling. But He was in the stern, asleep on a pillow. And they awoke Him and said to Him, "Teacher, do You not care that we are perishing?" Then He arose and rebuked the wind, and said to the sea, "Peace, be still!" And the wind ceased and there was a great calm. But He said to them, "Why are you so fearful? How is it that you have no faith?"
>
> —Mark 4:37–40

In this example about faith, rest can be used to help people understand that rest in Jesus can be viewed simply by believing everything he is in spite of unexpected challenges that arise during the journey of discovering their purpose in the day-of process. After Jesus quieted the storm, he asked his followers why they were so fearful and how it was that they had no faith. Jesus asked these questions to help his followers understand the day-of process. Jesus chose to sleep to demonstrate to others that he was waiting for them to see him for who he is—their only source of strength. Jesus sleeping on a pillow was a rest phase in hope that others would learn that he is who he says he is and as the Scripture has said. He wants everyone to know that faith empowers people to rest in who he is, especially when working becomes ineffective.

In 2 Samuel 5 under God's instructions, David defeated the Philistines. As a result, the Philistines regrouped and deployed once again in an attempt to defeat him. David prayed to the Lord asking whether he should fight the Philistines again and whether God would give him the victory by delivering them into his hand. The Lord's response to David's prayer was yes! However, the second set of instructions required work and a phase of rest. Although the resting phase is believing that what God did before he can do again, there are times when God will have people seek rest in his word differently from before.

> Then the Philistines went up once again and deployed themselves in the Valley of Rephaim. Therefore David inquired of the LORD, and He said, "You shall not go up; circle around behind them, and come upon them in front of the mulberry trees. And it shall be, when you hear the sound of marching in the tops of the mulberry trees, then you shall advance quickly. For then the LORD will go out before you to strike the camp of the Philistines." And David did so, as the LORD commanded him; and he drove back the Philistines from Geba as far as Gezer.
>
> —2 Sam. 5:22–25

Resting is a form of worship in which true worshippers relax in the knowledge of who God is. This worship will cultivate a more intimate, personal relationship with him. The quality of worship is determined by the weight of knowing who God is from a personal relationship and intimate experiences with him. True worshippers must leave behind circumstances from the past and seek the truth, which is knowing who God is regardless of challenging circumstances. Truth is seeking who he is in every circumstance.

*And when you pray, do not use vain repetitions as the heathen
do. For they think that they will be heard for their many words.
Therefore do not be like them. For your Father knows the things
you have need of before you ask Him.*

—Matt. 6:7–8

It's important for individuals to know that any luggage packed with such things as complicated situations, circumstances, and relationships cannot negatively affect or redefine a person's destiny. This is not the same as extra baggage where the weight of it becomes a challenge for individuals pursuing their destiny. Nevertheless, luggage carried on the journey contains things that people choose to bring with them to live life with purpose, such as jobs, education, personal health, marriage, family, and other cares of this world. Luggage, unlike extra baggage, can be thought-provoking during the journey of living life with purpose; however, luggage will never keep a person from living life with purpose. There are things, though, that can place people at risk for losing sight of their purpose—one such thing is having their luggage distract them from their destiny. God will spend the holy spirit to assist with a follower's thought process in keeping the luggage in its proper place as a part of living life on purpose and not as the purpose for their destination. Several years ago, my youngest daughter and I were returning from a vacation in Puerto Rico. We were waiting for our luggage in the baggage claim area, but it failed to arrive. I filled out all the necessary forms to claim my luggage. Although my luggage was to be delivered at a set date and time, the delay of my luggage did not keep me from reaching home as my final destination. When luggage becomes a challenge in getting you to your destiny, consider it to be extra baggage, and it's time to let it go! Don't let the luggage you choose to carry as part of your journey turn into unnecessary baggage. The truth of the matter is this: your luggage cannot control or dictate your destiny, destination, or purpose; it simply represents the things you choose to carry along the way to live life with purpose. Jesus is the process, the way to the process, and the one who calls people into the process. Don't allow the stuff in your luggage such as your place of work, relationships, finances, and religion become bigger in your mind than your destiny or purpose. Imagine sitting next to an individual and all they talk about is what they packed in their luggage, but they show little interest about where they are destined to go. Could it be as followers of Jesus Christ that what we have in our luggage has become more valuable than what we were created to do concerning purpose? In my travels, most people don't talk about what they packed in their luggage; rather, they are more focused on their destination. Followers having this similar mindset will find themselves feeding their purpose because it is what's feeding them, not the stuff they carry as luggage.

"God is Spirit, and those who worship Him must worship in spirit and truth" (John 4:24). To worship God in spirit is to be in his presence while believing in who he says he is as truth. Faith replaces the believer's perception about his or her circumstance with truth, knowing that the circumstance must submit to who God is. When looking for a place to worship God, believers must be guided by the Holy Spirit, and truth must be the pathway toward it. However, the place of worship is further within a believer's heart and mindset, not limited to a physical structure but illuminated by an understanding of who God is. "So Abraham took the wood of the burnt offering and laid it on Isaac his son; and he took the fire in his hand, and a knife, and the two of them went together" (Genesis 22:6).

There is a huge difference between truth and facts. Unlike faith, facts are usually things that we see with the natural eye. We can process information that seems factual. However, truth is understood through our spiritual eyes. Faith stands above all facts. For followers who desire a more intimate view of worship, a portion of the Lord's prayer can best illustrate the value of worship: "Our Father in heaven, hallowed be Your name. Your kingdom comes. Your will be done on earth as it is in heaven. Give us this day our daily bread" (Mathew 6:9–11). The Lord's prayer is not only an example of how to talk with God, but how to worship God in our conversation as well. An effective way of starting any communication with God is to first establish and acknowledge who

God is. God is a regulator over creations and particularly the things that personally affect the purpose of a believer. Believing this fosters a place of true worship. The people in the Bible who sought after Jesus with a great need for change frequently acknowledged who he was first as Lord, Master, and the Son of God. They perceived him not as Mary's son or the son of a carpenter but who he is as it relates to his purpose (I Am). They believed that if their outcome was to change, it would come through him and not what was known or considered to be tradition. They were able to see Jesus and his purpose. This mindset kept them from placing Jesus in a box that would have limited their faith from developing further. It is God who is waiting for people to see him in his purpose and how he intentionally has their steps prearranged toward their destiny. However, the challenge for some of us is that we sometimes forget who God is—that he is the author and finisher of our faith concerning our purpose.

I remember as a young person how my mother chastised me. With one hand raised in the air, exposing only the back of her hand because she knew it would deliver her correction much quicker, she would yell, "Do you know who you are talking to?" I didn't understand at that time, but my mother was telling me that the way I was thinking, which led to my talking back to her disrespectfully, was an ineffective way of communicating with her. When she raised that question, she was pointing out that I must have forgotten who she was as an authority figure and a true representation of the resurrection and life equipped to determine the consequences of my choices. Too often we forget, or we simply do not know, who we are talking to when we talk with God. Knowing who God is transforms our conversations from speaking to him to speaking with him:

> *Now when Jesus had entered Capernaum, a centurion came to Him, pleading with Him, saying, "Lord, my servant is lying at home paralyzed, dreadfully tormented." And Jesus said to him, "I will come and heal him." The centurion answered and said, "Lord, I am not worthy that You should come under my roof. But*

*only speak a word, and my servant will be healed. For I also am
a man under authority, having soldiers under me. And I say to
this one, 'Go,' and he goes; and to another, 'Come,' and he comes;
and to my servant, 'Do this,' and he does it." When Jesus heard
it, He marveled, and said to those who followed, "Assuredly, I
say to you, I have not found such great faith, not even in Israel."*

—Matt. 8:5–10

"Then Jesus said to the centurion, 'Go your way; and as you have
believed, so let it be done for you.' And his servant was healed that
same hour" (Matthew 8:13). This mindset establishes the rules of
engagement—that all things must submit to God simply because he
is God. The follower's belief system must come forth with boldness in
God as the power source in the day-of process, and as the daily bread.

Our daily bread is his grace, which supplies everything needed for
the day-of process. Our daily bread is God's grace for his creations to
live life and to live more abundantly toward purpose. In addition to
the rules of engagement in the day-of process, every so often, a sound
check is required to ensure that the plans are perfectly aligned with
God's plans in pursuit of purpose. "So David inquired of the LORD,
saying, 'Shall I go up against the Philistines? Will You deliver them into
my hand?' And the LORD said to David, 'Go up, for I will doubtless
deliver the Philistines into your hand'" (2 Samuel 5:19). Every so often
as followers, a sound check should be done to confirm alignment with
the Holy Spirit.

Jesus is mighty in strength and becomes the strength of believers
in their season of weakness: "My grace is sufficient for you, for My
strength is made perfect in weakness" (2 Corinthians 12:9). God does
his best work in our weak, complicated circumstances. Through these
periods, believers are made strong through his grace and by his spirit.
In the Lord's prayer, believers are asking, "Lord, give us this day our
daily bread." The Lord imparts the knowledge, by faith, that he is their
supplier on a daily basis. Because God is omniscient, he is aware that days
will vary and that life often presents itself with unexpected challenges.

The personal, intimate relationship that God desires with people creates a foundation that facilitates worship. This concept gives rise to a better understanding when God states, "This is the day the Lord has made; let us rejoice and be glad in it." True worshippers learn to appreciate the strategy that God uses in ordering their steps and not limiting their appreciation of the end results that flow from the first step. In other words, true worshippers acknowledge God while in the process rather than waiting to acknowledge him after obtaining the end result. "Declaring the end from the beginning, and from ancient times things that are not yet done" (Isaiah 46:10). True worshippers start worshipping God in the very beginning of the day the Lord has made, no matter the distance between that day and the rejoicing and being glad. Mark 4:37–39 speaks about a great windstorm that arose as Jesus was in the stern, asleep on a pillow, when his followers awakened him and asked if he cared about them as they faced an unexpectedly dangerous storm. As true worshippers, their understanding of this is the day the Lord has made let them be glad and rejoice in it and ensured that the day or circumstance never became their focal point. The revelation of who God is and the plans that he has for people to succeed in the struggle enable them to be glad and rejoice in it.

True worshippers understand when they believe Jesus is at rest in their circumstance; he already knows how the day is going to end. This type of faith empowers true worshippers in not seeing Jesus in every circumstance while knowing who he is in every circumstance and or struggle they face. Jesus wants people to know how to rest in spite of what the day appears to be in the beginning. God's plans include the beginning and the middle of each day he has made, which is why he encourages people to rejoice and to be glad in it because they have not seen the end. It is this mindset that fosters people to proclaim that the struggle often noted in the process of knowing Jesus as the word and that his word is worth the struggle. "Eye has not seen, nor ear heard, nor have entered into the heart of man the things which God has prepared for those who love Him" (1 Corinthians 2:9).

The distance or gap between this is the day the Lord has made and let us rejoice and be glad in it is found in opportunities to worship him. Worship is the key that grants you access to him. Faith is the key that opens the door to worship and works as a conduit that channels the truth of who God is before the manifestation of an answered prayer. People are placed where God takes up his residency. He is always searching for people who will worship him in every situation, be it good, bad, or indifferent. He is not limited to buildings such as churches or prayer closets: he is in every place. Make a joyful noise unto the Lord.

Believers soon learn the value of light in dark situations through the realization that the struggle is worth it. God uses the dark situations to teach the value of light to believers learning to walk by faith and not by the limitation of the natural eye. If it wasn't for the dark periods and leaps of faith during purpose development, the light coming from believers would be less effective in making a difference in the lives of others who are searching for that light. The role of darkness in the struggle for transformation from one's old way of thinking to having a mindset of Jesus helps people to know their purpose in such places as spiritual darkrooms. However, the light is kept from shining until they have become fully developed in the process of living life with purpose. The transformation process prepares people to think like Jesus. This thought process is the key to the kingdom of heaven and the gateway to being born again. It is in this state of mind that the born-again experience helps people to live what they were called to do according to God's purpose. Transformation of a new way of thinking and the born-again process are accomplished by a personal relationship with God through Jesus, not religion.

It can be very frustrating for some to be called and chosen to be a light to the world and not shine. At times in the journey, people will follow the facts and not the truth. When you latch on to the truth, faith opens its door toward worship. Before the light can be used for dark places in the world, it must be turned on from the inside before shining on the outside. Many people prefer to work with a light on, but in a spiritual darkroom, faith does its best work. Faith requires works in collaboration regardless of where the believer is in the process toward destiny. Entering a spiritual darkroom as a believer is a good reason to rejoice and be glad in it, for this is where the substance of faith begins to take shape and where people learn to trust a God they cannot see.

God is spirit. He must be worshipped in spirit and in truth. We are created in his likeness; therefore, he must be worshipped in spirit. Truth is the acknowledgment of who God is in the process of discovering our purpose regardless of the circumstance. Truth is faith existing in dark places. In this same place, revelation of purpose becomes illuminated for them to see evidence that what was hoped for was always on God's radar for development. God instructs his followers to come into the kingdom of heaven and its righteousness so that they may know who he is. Knowing who God is and his righteousness provides followers with the tools to see him in dark places, particularly when coping with complicated issues. From time to time, followers will have encounters with God but never know him intimately until they seek first the kingdom of God and its righteousness.

God is intentional. He proclaims that we are to have an expectancy or hope in his intentions. In Matthew 16:19, God promised that he will give the keys of the kingdom of heaven to his followers so that whatever they bind on earth will be bound in heaven, and whatever they loose on earth will be loosed in heaven. His will as it is in heaven shall be done here on earth. God's revelation of himself as he is in heaven is not intended to be a mystery to followers who seek first the kingdom of heaven and his righteousness. God has a plan and has promises for followers who seek him with a pure heart. Seeking who God is can only be done through Jesus who helps followers to discover how to live, move, and have their being in him. This wisdom gives rise to a better understanding of who God is. It also reveals the provisions God has put aside to support and aid the purpose he has called them to do. Knowing who God is empowers followers to know that all things are possible. This encourages and stirs up the faith within them to believe in the impossible and to understand that nothing is too hard for God.

One of the biggest benefits of seeking first the kingdom of God and its righteousness is getting to know who God is through Jesus. Consequently, developing a close, intimate relationship with Jesus can provide individuals with opportunities to know who God is. That personal relationship empowers followers to have faith in God and to believe that he can do the impossible. The process of seeking an intimate relationship gives followers access to the faith (Jesus) required to do the impossible. Seeking first the kingdom of God makes followers rich in him and not in the discovery of the things that are added after seeking the kingdom of God.

The kingdom of heaven resides within us. Seeking it requires unwrapping and removing the stuff that keeps us from knowing the kingdom of God and its righteousness within us. This is one of the reasons that seeking first the kingdom of God and his righteousness is such a mystery. Many people choose not to go through the process of removing the wrappings for some of it feels like a wall between who we think we are and how God sees our true identity. When your mind has not been transformed into having the same mindset that is in Jesus, it becomes very easy to think that obtaining the kingdom of God and its righteousness is more valuable than seeking it. Through seeking, we gain knowledge; the appreciation of this knowledge supports wisdom. Understanding how God thinks and what moves his heart has to be the believer's objective, not the possession of the kingdom of God or the stuff that comes with being associated with the kingdom. "Wisdom is the principal thing; therefore get wisdom: and with all thy getting get understanding" (Proverbs 4:7 KJV).

People are often faced with the struggle of learning to trust God in the process in discovering and living their purpose. In hindsight, the best lessons I learned in the struggle of discovering and living my purpose is when I found myself tripping over the fact that I thought I knew what was best in seeing how change should take place rather than trusting God's ordered steps in the transformation process. The most challenging experience in the process of living life with purpose is the transformation from a mindset that doesn't align with Jesus's thoughts to a mindset that thinks like his. Understanding God's faithfulness and his commitment to his word was where I first believed that God not only designed the process but is I AM for the people in the process; moreover, he is the process. "Jesus said to him, 'I am the way, the truth, and the life. No one comes to the Father except through Me'" (John 14:6). It was his word that promised me a purpose that would succeed; although, at times, I struggled through it. It never ceases to amaze me that every time I said no to God along the way toward destiny, he remained faithful to everything he had spoken about my purpose in spite of the consequences of my poor choices. As a follower, the greatest achievement in the struggle is to learn patiently how to trust God in the process and look to him as the process. "Knowing that the testing of your faith produces patience. But let patience have its perfect work, that you may be perfect and complete, lacking nothing" (James 1:3–4).

Currency is often defined as a form of circulation used as a medium for trade. What we consider to be money here on earth is a type of currency often used for an exchange of things; however, money as a form of currency cannot be used in the kingdom of God. Faith in the kingdom of God is the only type of currency that is allowed to be used for exchange for everything that God has to provide; often it comes in the form of a seed.

> *Then He said, "To what shall we liken the kingdom of God? Or with what parable shall we picture it? It is like a mustard seed which, when it is sown on the ground, is smaller than all the seeds on earth; but when it is sown, it grows up and becomes greater than all herbs, and shoots out large branches, so that the birds of the air may nest under its shade."*
>
> —Mark 4:30–33

God is sharing with his readers and those who hear the word that faith as a seed will give access to the core of who he is. Those who believe in him, and as he said, according to his written word, become empowered in wisdom and understanding. When people seek first the kingdom of

God and its righteousness, it becomes an expression in a believer's life that God's mode of operation in the kingdom is the way for them to live, move, and have their being as it is in heaven and on earth. One of the principles that God uses in his kingdom when one seeks his presence is seedtime and harvest. Faith, process, and God's promises work similar to seedtime and harvest, and this information empowers believers to understand why God incorporated process as a mode of operation. This type of mindset will assist others in appreciating the ordered steps for their lives and life itself. "While the earth remains, seedtime and harvest, cold and heat, winter and summer, and day and night shall not cease" (Genesis 8:22).

The joy in understanding the importance of the process empowers followers to grow into a closer, more intimate relationship with God through Jesus. The process plays a vital role in your destiny because it provides the tools needed to function in your purpose. God exposed the end before the beginning to his followers as a strategic plan to initiate the process of seeking the things that have to be learned to reach the finished product. Case in point: it's not the end result, such as receiving a college degree, that warrants a celebration of achievement, but it is what you went through to get that degree that prompts the celebration. The cherry on the cake is not ultimately reaching the kingdom of God; rather, it is about the things you learn throughout the journey that helped you to know who God is. Moreover, in preparation for this journey, faith works to develop and equip us for the appointed time.

There is an old saying I often heard while growing up in a large church family: "It's the squeaky worshipper that gets the attention." A squeaky worshipper or a true worshipper is not limited by the loud sounds that come from his or her mouth in worship, but by an enlarged heart in seeking who God is in the journey while understanding the struggles in the process. Squeaky worshippers become loud by acknowledging God for making the necessary changes in their hearts to create room for him to expand. Squeaky worshippers see the change as worth the struggle rather than questioning God about the need for change. It is the heart condition of a squeaky worshipper or true worshipper that quickly gets God's attention.

"There was a certain creditor who had two debtors. One owed five hundred denarii, and the other fifty. And when they had nothing with which to repay, he freely forgave them both. Tell Me, therefore, which of them will love him more?" Simon answered and said, 'I suppose the one whom he forgave more.'"

—Luke 7:41–43

A squeaky worshipper is one who is grateful for the debt paid in full by Jesus at the cross. The squeaky worshipper is relentless in worship. It is the Holy Spirit who creates the space in the hearts of people to increase in size for God to reveal who he is as King of kings. Although the debtors have been forgiven, the debt, their gratitude, creates a greater space in their hearts for the one who has done much for them. Squeaky worshippers believe in giving God his well-deserved praise and acknowledgment for who he is. Worshippers develop a better understanding of and appreciation for the strategy that God uses for process. Knowing who God is makes the struggle worth pursuing rather than questioning why some steps come with struggles when one is headed toward destiny. Squeaky worshippers can get God's attention more quickly because their focus is on who God is as it relates to their purpose in the process and not where they are in the process. Acknowledging who God is in the transformation process is a demonstration of faith that implies that we trust God before the process is completed simply because of who he is. Do you know that there is absolutely no one who knows you better, and no one who can better showcase your true identity than God? "Before I formed thee in the belly I knew thee; and before thou camest forth out of the womb I sanctified thee, and I ordained thee a prophet unto the nations" (Jeremiah 1:5 KJV).

How God perceives the process in preparing you is often misunderstood and very different from how others think it should be done when faced with struggles. Furthermore, when he sees our misperceptions toward challenges, he doesn't always remove the challenge that stands in the way of pursuing our destiny. But he will instruct people to change the way they think toward any challenge affecting their pursuit toward purpose. Just as our steps are ordered, the things that we should think about are also ordered by God. He tells us in his word: Let the same mind that is in Jesus be also in you. How you think, or your perception of the process, dictates your reaction or response to the process. Whatever or however you think, your behavior follows it. The process for kingdom-seeking followers becomes a lifestyle rather than a period to pass through because you have learned to wait in God and not for God. God is waiting for us to continue with the process. "And let us not grow weary while doing good, for in due season we shall reap if we do not lose heart" (Galatians 6:9). God is waiting for us to become empty so he can fill us with his spirit in the pursuit of discovering purpose in spite of the struggle of running on empty.

RUNNING ON EMPTY
IN THE STRUGGLE

CHAPTER 6

Serving as the primary caregivers for someone with a shortened life expectancy placed other family members and me at risk of having to struggle with running on empty. Bereavement has been defined in several research studies as consisting of five stages. Denial, anger, bargaining, depression, and acceptance are part of learning to cope with loss. These stages were first suggested by Elisabeth Kübler-Ross in her 1969 book *On Death and Dying*. The five stages are not stops on the way to recovering from grief, but at times, they are places of rest until the individual is ready to move to the next stage or revisit a previous stage. The stages of grief and mourning are accepted worldwide and are experienced by people of different ages, genders, religions, and cultures. Mourning occurs in response to an individual's own terminal illness, the loss of a close relationship, or the death of a person or animal. People often revisit stages before realizing a more peaceful understanding of death. Too often, people are not given the luxury of time needed to get to acceptance. They may find themselves running on empty before they arrive at the final stage.

Running on empty can lead individuals straight to Jesus to be made whole, and their only sense of true strength makes this struggle worth it. True worshippers understand that Jesus is the resurrection and the life when they are running on empty. In Jeremiah 29:11, God says, "For I know the thoughts that I think toward you, says the LORD, thoughts of peace and not of evil, to give you a future and a hope." This passage can be read as a promise from God that elevates one's level of believing. Not even death can threaten a believer's purpose or the plans that God has for him or her. Several people in the Bible ran on empty but saw their hope fulfilled by him. In spite of their challenges, they continued to press through to be made whole. They believed with all their hearts that Jesus is the pure substance of faith. To truly seek Jesus as the substance of faith is to purposely run on empty as this passage illustrates:

> *And a certain woman, which had an issue of blood twelve years, and had suffered many things of many physicians, and had spent all that she had, and was nothing bettered, but rather grew worse, when she had heard of Jesus, came in the press behind, and touched his garment. For she said, If I may touch but his clothes, I shall be whole. And straightway the fountain of her blood was dried up; and she felt in her body that she was healed of that plague. And Jesus, immediately knowing in himself that virtue had gone out of him, turned him about in the press, and said, Who touched my clothes? And his disciples said unto him, Thou seest the multitude thronging thee, and sayest thou, Who touched me? And he looked round about to see her that had done this thing. But the woman fearing and trembling, knowing what was done in her, came and fell down before him, and told him all the truth. And he said unto her, Daughter, thy faith hath made thee whole; go in peace and be whole of thy plague.*
>
> —Mark 5:25–34 KJV

While running on empty, this woman saw her journey toward Jesus as a pathway into seeing him for who he is. Before touching the hem of his garment, the Holy Spirit revealed to her who Jesus is. A revelation by faith was conceived, and when she heard and believed who Jesus is, conception took place at that moment, and she no longer had to run on empty. "So then faith comes by hearing, and hearing by the word of God" (Romans 10:17). Hearing that Jesus was coming was the catalyst that drew her into her journey. While she was pressing toward the crowd on empty to get to Jesus, she began to worship him. Her worship allowed her to rejoice and to be glad in the day the Lord had made. She knew there would be just a small window of opportunity to touch the hem of his garment, but because she was aligned with Jesus, her recovery, which appeared impossible for 12 years, suddenly became possible. This woman, while running on empty, was able to ignore her illness just enough to see the revelation of who Jesus is, and as a result, she was empowered by faith to press toward the purpose of Jesus. The crowds surrounding Jesus were in position to touch him. Some also walked shoulder to shoulder with him, yet they could not see who he is as the son of God or his purpose. Although she was still sick, it was not until she worshipped Jesus by faith that she was able to bow down to his hem. In addition, she realized that she was not just healed, but she was made whole. It's one thing when Jesus gives life to an individual, and it's another when it is revealed to a person that Jesus is the resurrected who gives life to dead things. This woman did not become distracted by what she went through during the 12 years or by the challenge to touch the hem of his garment when she was running on empty. Her disorder was not 12 years of trying to get well but 12 years of walking toward her destiny, even when it seemed that she was losing everything and that life was slipping away from her. She moved from wanting to be healed to becoming whole. The things a person learns while going through the process toward destiny will move them from wanting to be healed to being made whole. "For everyone to whom much is given, from him much will be required" (Luke 12:48). What she had to go through in the process was necessary to move her to her destiny. "And we know that all things work together for good to those who love God, to those who are the called according to His purpose" (Romans 8:28).

"The eyes of your understanding being enlightened; that ye may know what is the hope of his calling, and what the riches of the glory of his inheritance in the saints" (Ephesians 1:18 KJV). This is where God becomes understood by people during the process of seeking first the kingdom of God and its righteousness while discovering their destiny. Once you understand God as it relates to purpose, you can be faithful toward God during the process before the appointed time. The big-ticket question is not what happens during the struggle but why it happens and how God will use it to prepare individuals for destiny. Too often, followers become distracted with their gifts and fail to stay focused on the process that prepares them for the appointed time to implement their gift or anointing. "And let us not grow weary while doing good, for in due season we shall reap if we do not lose heart" (Galatians 6:9). The tenacity of this woman came from her ability to keep her focus on who Jesus is and not on the last 12 years of coping with her bleeding disorder. She didn't allow what the people around her said to limit her. Although she was running on empty, she didn't allow even that to affect her date with destiny. Her position in life took a back seat to the mission of who Jesus is. Everything that transpired before she saw Jesus for who he is was part of the process that led her to her destination in receiving an abundant life. Many people touched Jesus throughout the day, but her touch caused Jesus to turn around and stop to acknowledge that the substance of her faith came from him.

Faith is the key that activates the story God reveals to believers who have a personal yet intimate relationship with Jesus. Since Jesus is the author and finisher of our faith, he is also the only one who can tell the story that leads to our destiny. As believers, we live out our story here on earth inasmuch as it is activated by faith. Jesus is both the storyteller and the key that gives life to the believer's story. Jesus is the words that God uses to create our purpose, and Jesus is the substance that gives life to the words used for believers to live the life he said we can. In believers seeking their true identity, Jesus increases, while what is less important to their purpose decreases.

For I know the thoughts that I think toward you, says the LORD, thoughts of peace and not of evil, to give you a future and a hope. Then you will call upon Me and go and pray to Me, and I will listen to you. And you will seek Me and find Me, when you search for Me with all your heart.

—Jeremiah 29:11–13

And she had a sister called Mary, who also sat at Jesus' feet and heard His word. But Martha was distracted with much serving, and she approached Him and said, "Lord, do You not care that my sister has left me to serve alone? Therefore tell her to help me." And Jesus answered and said to her, "Martha, Martha, you are worried and troubled about many things. But one thing is needed, and Mary has chosen that good part, which will not be taken away from her."

—Luke 10:39–43

Running on empty gives people the opportunity to choose to sit at the feet of Jesus. They see Jesus as their only source of life, and what he thinks gives life to them in believing in his word and in who he is. Mary found pleasure in being in Jesus's presence—not just sitting next to him but being in his presence to seek who he is. The Bible tells us that without faith, it is impossible to please God. Jesus is the core or substance of what faith is and should not be limited to the current mindset of who we think he is.

If believers really want to get God's attention, all they have to do is delight themselves merely by being in his presence. God absolutely enjoys when a believer becomes more interested in the strategy behind the scenes and does not limit God to the contents of the story. In short, God is looking for believers such as this Mary, who are willing to sit at the feet of Jesus and say, "Master, tell that story again, but this time tell me what you were thinking about when you wrote that part into the story."

Being in the presence of Jesus was an opportunity for Mary as a vessel to see the benefits of having the need to decrease areas of life that did not acknowledge Jesus's purpose. This opportunity allowed Jesus to fill her with living water, which transformed her mindset so much that she used a bottle filled with expensive ointment for the master's use:

And behold, a woman in the city who was a sinner, when she knew that Jesus sat at the table in the Pharisee's house, brought an alabaster flask of fragrant oil, and stood at His feet behind Him weeping; and she began to wash His feet with her tears, and wiped them with the hair of her head; and she kissed His feet and anointed them with the fragrant oil. Now when the Pharisee who had invited Him saw this, he spoke to himself, saying, "This Man, if He were a prophet, would know who and what manner of woman this is who is touching Him, for she is a sinner." And Jesus answered and said to him, "Simon, I have something to say to you." So, he said, "Teacher, say it." "There was a certain creditor who had two debtors. One owed five hundred denarii, and the other fifty. And when they had nothing with which to repay, he freely forgave them both. Tell Me, therefore, which of them will love him more?" Simon answered and said, "I suppose the one whom he forgave more." And He said to him, "You have rightly judged." Then He turned to the woman and said to Simon, "Do you see this woman? I entered your house; you gave Me no water for My feet, but she has washed My feet with her tears and wiped them with the hair of her head. You gave Me no kiss, but this woman has not ceased to kiss My feet since the time I came in. You did not anoint My head with oil, but this woman has anointed My feet with fragrant oil. Therefore, I say to you, her sins, which are many, are forgiven, for she loved much. But to whom little is forgiven, the same loves little."

—Luke 7:37–47

At the end of each day that the Lord has made when the rubber meets the road, that is the time to ask, "Am I closer in my thinking process to rejoicing and being glad in the day the Lord has made? Am I closer to Jesus than I was when I first started?" The answers to these questions are hidden in a personal yet intimate relationship with God and a mindset that thinks like Jesus. The key to having a personal relationship with God through Jesus is to empty out the storehouse. By emptying our storehouse, we decrease self-righteousness and are made right under his righteousness. As the mindset of who Jesus is increases in us, we become more accessible to our true identity and available for the master's use. This new way of thinking comes from a mindset or thought process that has been transformed to think like Jesus.

The woman with the issue of blood for 12 years headed toward Jesus for him to heal her spirit. She was running on empty knowing that only Jesus could fill her emptiness. She was anointed and directed by the Holy Spirit. She had a predetermined appointment to meet with the appointed time. God is faithful to those he has called, set aside, and prepared for appointed moments.

Both Mary and the woman who had the issue of blood for 12 years finally met up with their appointed time as they were running on empty emotionally, physically, and spiritually:

> On the last day, that great day of the feast, Jesus stood and cried out, saying, "If anyone thirsts, let him come to Me and drink. He who believes in Me, as the Scripture has said, out of his heart will flow rivers of living water."
>
> —John 7:37–38

The steps ordered by God are the same steps that take people into their destiny. These destiny steps are preordered because of his righteousness and not the self-righteousness of followers. Destiny steps, by the way of transformation, take people on a journey to discover their purpose upon knowing first who God is. These destiny steps in the process of transformation empower people to search for who God is while believing in him as their only provider toward uncovering purpose. "And He said to me, 'My grace is sufficient for you, for My strength is made perfect in weakness. Therefore, most gladly I will rather boast in my infirmities, that the power of Christ may rest upon me'" (2 Corinthians 12:9). "They are new every morning: great is thy faithfulness" (Lamentations 3:23 KJV). When running on empty, believers can expect to be stretched by Jesus during the transformation process as they are prepared to live in their purpose. While she was stretching, the woman with the issue of blood for 12 years was made whole in a destiny step grounded by faith. God's great faithfulness sees purpose, potential, and possibilities beyond all barriers that try to stop others from stretching toward their true identity and purpose.

> *Now Israel loved Joseph more than all his children, because he was the son of his old age. Also, he made him a tunic of many colors. But when his brothers saw that their father loved him more than all his brothers, they hated him and could not speak peaceably to him. Now Joseph had a dream, and he told it to his brothers; and they hated him even more.*
>
> —Gen. 37:3–5

Genesis 39:11–21 shares how Joseph was pursued by his master's wife and wrongly accused of something he didn't do because his commitment to God was much stronger than what anyone could give him or threaten him with. Joseph faced adversities, such as personal relationship issues with his brothers who left him in a pit to be sold as a slave and being sentenced to jail by false accusations from Potiphar's wife. These adversities caused him to spend many years in jail, but he knew that his gift was from God and that God's favor among Israel would get him from the pit to a position in the palace where he could further live his purpose. Through it all, God never removed the gift and the favor he gave Joseph, nor did he remove his adversities. God's gifts are wrapped in promises and secured with goodness and mercy. In spite of how Joseph's brothers felt about him and how maliciously they treated him, God's goodness and mercy taught him to forgive his brothers and those who wrongfully accused him of something he did not do. The promises of God can turn everything meant for evil into a more pleasant outcome for followers who learn to trust him while facing adversities. Joseph, his family, and many communities became beneficiaries for years to come because God took their emptiness and filled it with who he is in spite of adversities.

God is waiting for others to run on empty. Challenging circumstances often will pave the way for others to run on empty: "But those who wait on the LORD shall renew their strength; they shall mount up with wings like eagles, they shall run and not be weary, they shall walk and not faint" (Isaiah 40:31). Having a mindset like Jesus is to empty out the old way of thinking and doing things. When believers run on empty and desire to be transformed by renewing their old way of thinking, that excites and pleases God. God waits for followers to run on empty with the hope that their storehouse is empty and open for what he has to offer as it relates to having a new mindset. The type of emptiness that God seeks is where the substance of faith transforms people from what they have come to understand in their old way of thinking into having a thought process like Jesus. Rejoicing and being glad in the day the Lord has made is a way of proclaiming to God that your storehouse, as it relates to your old thought process, is now empty and that there is room to think like Jesus. In the process of discovering one's purpose, God is looking not just for followers or believers but anyone who is looking for more than just a favor from God or man. He is looking for people with a deep desire in their hearts to push their purpose to fruition and to go after the thing that has never been done before. Moreover, followers are relentlessly willing to have their labor induced. For these individuals, adversities are used to break their water for life to flow out.

In my last pregnancy, my water broke on its own; the first seven births were induced to aid the delivery process. In each of my first seven pregnancies, I was in painful active labor for what felt like several hours of torture; my doctor told me that I was over five centimeters dilated and that it would be best to use an instrument to break my water to speed up the process. Sometimes, God will induce our labor or our readiness for purpose by breaking the water in the process of speeding up the birth to our purpose. Although many times God will speed up the labor process, he will not omit the discomfort that comes with the process. I took Lamaze classes because I thought Lamaze would work as a form of coping with my pain during labor and delivery. What I learned was that it wasn't the Lamaze classes that taught me how to cope more effectively with pain, but it was the pain that I went through that prepared me for the next occurrence of pain in future deliveries. Pain and pleasure do not move God in the pursuit of purpose. He will use adversities to get the attention from others who may not know him as the only living and most mighty and powerful God. He is searching for people to see him as their only option and as midwife or facilitator to their purpose. This thinking fosters a belief that inducing the labor process makes purpose more effective. Asking God to induce the birth process for the believer to be more effective for his glory comes from worship. God is looking for anyone who is relentless about believing in who he is. In your pursuit of who he is, do not allow what others may say about your past or limitations to distract you or cause you to doubt God. Too often, a person will be challenged within the process so that his or her concerns are based on other people's perceptions in their struggle toward destiny, not on seeking first the kingdom of God to find the path that is preordered toward destiny. Often, in seeking the kingdom of heaven first, we experience both the pain and the pleasure of knowing who God is. The pain is often associated with removing things that we consider to be the norm or okay; the pleasure often follows after space or room has been made for God to get the glory.

A couple of summers ago, I prepared some leftover curry chicken to take to work. It was a very hot day, and the minute I got to the hospital, I was busy providing health-care services to patients on my unit. It was so busy that I wasn't able to eat dinner until nine o'clock that night. When I went to get my dinner, I remembered that I had left it out on the counter at the nurses' station. I never put it in the refrigerator. I opened the container and smelled my dinner. It smelled fine, so I ate it. On my way home from work at midnight, I felt sick to my stomach. I ran upstairs to my apartment and headed for the bathroom, where my body worked to get rid of what I had eaten. My body, not my mind, was in full control. At times, the muscles in my throat were choking me when I believed my stomach was empty. At last, one large piece of chicken came out. At that moment, I became well and regained control over my body, and my mind had a say. Pain and pleasure are tools in God's strategy toward exposing purpose. The pain of being sick to my stomach and losing control of my body was necessary for me to have the pleasure of being well.

> *And whenever the time came for Elkanah to make an offering, he would give portions to Peninnah his wife and to all her sons and daughters. But to Hannah he would give a double portion, for he loved Hannah, although the LORD had closed her womb. And her rival also provoked her severely, to make her miserable, because the LORD had closed her womb. So it was, year by year, when she went up to the house of the LORD, that she provoked her; therefore she wept and did not eat.*
>
> —1 Sam. 1:4–7

> *Then Elkanah her husband said to her, "Hannah, why do you weep? Why do you not eat? And why is your heart grieved? Am I not better to you than ten sons?" So, Hannah arose after they had finished eating and drinking in Shiloh. Now Eli the priest was sitting on the seat by the doorpost of the tabernacle of the LORD. And she was in bitterness of soul and prayed to the LORD and wept in anguish. Then she made a vow and said, "O LORD of hosts, if You will indeed look on the affliction of Your maidservant and remember me, and not forget Your maidservant, but will give Your maidservant a male child."*
>
> —1 Sam. 1:8–11

Then they rose early in the morning and worshiped before the LORD, and returned and came to their house at Ramah. And Elkanah knew Hannah his wife, and the LORD remembered her. So it came to pass in the process of time that Hannah conceived and bore a son, and called his name Samuel, saying, "Because I have asked for him from the LORD."

—1 Sam. 1:19–20

Because of Hannah's intimate relationship with God, her breakthrough took place at the temple. She gave birth to her son, Samuel, but she also gave birth to the realization that all things are possible in God. Hannah's destiny was birth in spite of her pain, confusion, being misunderstood by others, and feeling disconnected from her purpose. Her pain, disconnection, and discontent allowed her to run on empty and pushed Hannah to her destiny. Clearly, Hannah had the favor of God and her husband. However, it wasn't until she was running on empty that she came into the position to discover her purpose and that the struggle was worth it. Hannah needed more than just favor from God and her husband; she needed God to do a new thing by opening a door that she thought was closed—a door that only God could open. In discovering purpose, running on empty becomes essential. When you feel you are in the struggle and at the end of your rope, God will demonstrate his mercy and goodness by inducing labor for the sake of the appointed time. This crazy, relentless love pushed Hannah to the next level in her relationship with God. Believing he was the only one who could do it, in her struggle, she first had to run on empty; in retrospect, the struggle was worth it.

God's grace gives believers and, sometimes people who are not religiously connected, total access to the secret places of God. This is the place where they can come boldly to his resting place and make their request known to him. This place allows followers to walk away in perfect peace knowing that it was not their self-righteousness that granted their request; it was being in the right relationship or plugged in with God that empowered them to receive their blessing. This intimate place in the mindset of followers and others inspires them to realize that a crumb from the king's table is more than enough to change the game. God is waiting for people to arrive at a level in their thinking beyond being saved where they are totally committed to give him back everything that he put in them by becoming like-minded in Jesus. Philippians 2:7–9 describes Jesus this way:

> *But made Himself of no reputation, taking the form of a bondservant, and coming in the likeness of men. And being found in appearance as a man, He humbled Himself and became obedient to the point of death, even the death of the cross. Therefore, God also has highly exalted him and given him the name which is above every name.*

God listens to the voice of a true worshipper who gives thanks for the process before receiving the promise. He continues to wait for anyone to call out his name and believe that all things are possible because he is the God of all possibilities. Being grateful for what God has done is one thing, but for a follower to be grateful for the process before fruition is a whole new level of worship. Acknowledging the process gives God the glory for his creative strategy and careful craftsmanship in the gifts he placed inside a believer before he formed them in their mother's womb. Acknowledging God empowers the ability to be glad in the day the Lord has made. As followers, we can thank God for who he is before any outcome or promise comes. This level of awareness opens the door to his inner courts and to the heart of God.

When Hannah was at the temple crying out to God, she was worshipping God, which caused her to go into a spiritual labor. Hannah's relationship with God led her to the secret place where God rests. This place was inside the temple of her worship where Hannah felt a pulling inside her spirit, leading her in perfect alignment with him so he could pull out of her what he put into her.

> *The LORD kills and makes alive; He brings down to the grave and brings up. The LORD makes poor and makes rich; He brings low and lifts up. He raises the poor from the dust and lifts the*

beggar from the ash heap, to set them among princes and make them inherit the throne of glory.

—1 Sam. 2:6–8

Although Hannah knew that the favor of God was in her life, her request needed God to intercede on her behalf and go beyond favor. God is waiting for people to request a personal, supernatural intervention on their behalf, something that surpasses favor.

However, faith should not stop here. The next level of faith is becoming the cheerful giver, and like Hannah, giving your gift from God back to him. For example, take the one leper who returned to Jesus to say thank you. God is looking for followers who trust him more than the gift that we ask for and who are willing to give it back to him simply because our relationship with him is greater and much bigger than the gift itself. This mindset feeds the lifestyle of a true worshipper. The value is not in the thing that God has given you but the God who stands by the thing he placed in you. God instructs us that we are to seek first the kingdom of heaven and its righteousness and all things shall be added to us. Hannah wanted a son, but she realized in her relationship with God that she had to seek the kingdom of God first and its righteousness and to trust God that the thing she requested would come to pass. Hannah got into an alignment with her destiny as part of the labor process before pushing and pressing toward the birth of her purpose. This process of pressing and pushing is often a struggle, but it is necessary for followers to see themselves as the solution or answer to a problem or question. Too often, followers see their circumstances as problematic and not in preparation for a solution created by God's design to fix the problems. Hannah's breakthrough came to fruition when she believed in her heart that all things are possible in spite of her current situation of infertility. She used her purpose to be part of a solution concerning Israel and the destiny God had placed on her.

But to Hannah he would give a double portion, for he loved Hannah, although the LORD had closed her womb. And her rival also provoked her severely, to make her miserable, because the LORD had closed her womb. So it was, year by year, when she went up to the house of the LORD, that she provoked her; therefore she wept and did not eat.

—1 Sam. 1:5–8

Several years before meeting Jerry, my first marriage ended in divorce. I began dating and sleeping with almost any man I thought was worth looking at. My self-esteem had hit rock bottom. At that time, I was a single mother of five children. Although saved and set aside for the master's use and having God's favor, I was struggling to seek my true identity and purpose. My greatest fear was getting pregnant without having a husband with a sense of family. I struggled with fornication so much that I chose to have a relationship with it rather than stopping it. I got on my knees in tears and begged God to take away my ability to get pregnant. In 1993, I met Jerry at our place of work, and we were married in 1994. For three years, we were not able to conceive a child, though we were both considered healthy and vibrant people. We tried everything, and finally we saw a doctor who specialized in infertility.

Now, keep in mind that I was already blessed and highly favored by God by having five children all under the age of 12, but I wanted to have more children with Jerry. In 1997, Jerry and I were becoming increasingly frustrated, and he began to blame himself. That's when I recalled the favor God had given me years earlier during my struggle with fornication. I told Jerry that the problem was neither him nor me. I told him I had to go to God alone and ask him to undo the request that I asked of him several years earlier. I went to my room and got on my knees and asked God for mercy but with thanksgiving for his covering and favor throughout the years. I told God that I didn't have any righteousness of my own, because fornication had been a struggle in my life, but that I knew that the God I served even while in sin is merciful, kind, loving, and powerful. I additionally believed that he would and could speak to the dry areas of my life and resurrect my barren womb. Needless to say, I got pregnant and continued to have babies until I was 42. The struggle I had with fornication empowered me to know that the struggle was worth it because it empowered me to know a God who can close doors that no man can open and open doors that no man can close. God was more touched by how I believed in who I saw him to be in my struggle with fornication and not that I am a fornicator. The challenge with fornication became worth the struggle because I saw God's mercy and grace while I was still in sin.

Jerry and I had three children together after trying everything for three years from health-care professionals to get pregnant with no success. Similar to Hannah, I got on my knees and remembered in my struggle who God is. From this experience with God, I've learned that he is willing to give people more than just his favor. What made it so great was that he covered my ineffective righteousness with the righteousness of Jesus. Jerry and I had three children supernaturally versus using fertility drugs. As a result, my last three children are two years apart, just like my first five children. Because of God's faithfulness, I gave them back to him by naming them Joshua, Caleb, and Althea.

> *Then she made a vow and said, "O Lord of hosts, if You will indeed look on the affliction of Your maidservant and remember me, and not forget Your maidservant, but will give Your maidservant a male child, then I will give him to the Lord all the days of his life."*
>
> —1 Sam. 1:11

In the day the Lord has made, God's grace will always be sufficient. I was a hot mess. I am still a hot mess in my eyes, but his grace and mercy will always have my back. Hannah's steps and my steps in discovering our true identity in God were different. But the personal relationships we shared with God were similar because we believed that when our desperation met God's grace, all things were made possible. God waits patiently for people who just happen to feel desperate to ask him to bring out the things he planted in them and the promises that guarantee them success. Even though I am an empty vessel, there are days when I see myself more than just an empty vessel for the master's use. I see myself as mashed potatoes, beef stew, a platter of fresh fried fish, a tossed dark green leafy salad, steamed and seasoned rice and peas, collard greens, barbecue ribs, string beans, baked beans, baked macaroni and cheese, cornbread, yeast rolls, grilled and fried chicken, homemade apple pie, and peach cobbler pie—all of this and more coming from this one vessel simply because I am filled with knowing who God is.

Followers may have two conflicting thoughts: knowing you're an empty vessel for the master's use but having a vital belief that deep within lies a buffet of food.

> *Taking the five loaves and the two fish and looking up to heaven, he gave thanks and broke the loaves. Then he gave them to the disciples, and the disciples gave them to the people. They all ate and were satisfied, and the disciples picked up twelve basketfuls of broken pieces that were left over.*
>
> —Matt. 14:19–20 NIV

God is not limited to what he gave you to eat yesterday. Because he is omnipresent, omniscient, and all-powerful, he can take the least and feed people and have several baskets of leftovers because his grace is more than enough.

My children, family members, and other loved ones are all witness to the fact that when we have a family gathering at my house, I prepare a feast for a king. My kids come to my house with empty containers knowing there will be more than enough for them to take home and have at least two or more meals for that week when they get home. This is the same concept God has for his children when he prepares a feast for them from his word. We as his children are to take leftovers from his table and feed others.

I believe God's good intention for the world is for believers to be fishers of men by using what he has given to feed others from his table. This becomes an opportunity for people to believe in the living bread (Jesus) who can change their current path by revealing to them their true identity. Without God, I am just an empty vessel, but with him, I am a belly of living water and a banquet created to feed hundreds of hungry people searching for who God is as the great I Am.

When God puts his promises and anointings on people, he does not limit his gifts to that one individual or group of people, but he sees and uses the leftovers to be blessings for many. God is generational and futuristic in all his planning and the implementation of his plans. God is looking for people who can dream beyond themselves, beyond their immediate neighborhood, beyond their culture and gender. "For God so loved the world that He gave His only begotten Son, that whoever believes in Him should not perish but have everlasting life" (John 3:16). God is looking not just for believers or followers but for anyone willing to see the world as a place to serve his word as fresh-cooked, ready-to-eat food to all people. Moreover, he seeks those who are willing to lose the mindset of just serving the king's food to a select few. Each time believers attend church services or leave the presence of the Lord, they become the spiritual leftover bread that God expects them to give to others who are hungry for his word. Believers are not just the leftovers to be used for the master's service, but they are never to forget that he is the baker and the only supplier of bread that gives everlasting life. Although others also provide bread, their bread, unlike Jesus's bread, does not provide everlasting life, and it can be a distraction from the adversary for people who want everlasting life. Similar to the leftover bread from Jesus, the transformation process changes believers to become leftover bread of life to feed those who are hungry and wanting to live life more abundantly through him.

> *And he sighed deeply in his spirit, and saith, Why doth this generation seek after a sign? verily I say unto you, There shall no sign be given unto this generation. And he left them, and entering into the ship again departed to the other side. Now the disciples had forgotten to take bread, neither had they in the ship with them more than one loaf. And he charged them, saying, Take heed, beware of the leaven of the Pharisees, and of the leaven of Herod. And they reasoned among themselves,*

saying, It is because we have no bread. And when Jesus knew it, he saith unto them, Why reason ye, because ye have no bread? perceive ye not yet, neither understand? have ye your heart yet hardened? Having eyes, see ye not? and having ears, hear ye not? and do ye not remember? When I brake the five loaves among five thousand, how many baskets full of fragments took ye up? They say unto him, Twelve. And when the seven among four thousand, how many baskets full of fragments took ye up? And they said, Seven. And he said unto them, How is it that ye do not understand?

—Mark 8:12–21 KJV

Jesus answered them and said, "Most assuredly, I say to you, you seek Me, not because you saw the signs, but because you ate of the loaves and were filled. Do not labor for the food which perishes, but for the food which endures to everlasting life, which the Son of Man will give you, because God the Father has set His seal on Him." Then they said to Him, "What shall we do, that we may work the works of God?" Jesus answered and said to them, "This is the work of God, that you believe in Him whom He sent." Therefore, they said to Him, "What sign will You perform then, that we may see it and believe You? What work will You do? Our fathers ate the manna in the desert; as it is written, 'He gave them bread from heaven to eat.'" Then Jesus said to them, "Most assuredly, I say to you, Moses did not give you the bread from heaven, but My Father gives you the true bread from heaven. For the bread of God is He who comes down from heaven and gives life to the world." Then they said to Him, "Lord, give us this bread always." And Jesus said to them, "I am the bread of life. He who comes to Me shall never hunger, and he who believes in Me shall never thirst."

—John 6:26–35

The day the Lord has made is all about God drawing people into having an intimate, personal relationship with him through the means of process. It is a day that offers opportunities for people to choose the one who first chose to love them through relationship and not religion. Worship is a by-product of knowing who God is.

To be absent from the body is to be present in the Lord. Seek to know how God sees you in your daily circumstances and not how you or the world sees you. Everything, including daily challenges, is part of the process of drawing people into a closer relationship to God as his beloved children. Seeking God and his righteousness unveils believers as partners in who Jesus is. Seeking who God is establishes a relationship with Jesus that reveals a follower's true identity. This revelation becomes the follower's true reflection of who Jesus is in their steps, their purpose, and throughout the process.

Have the same mind in you that is in Christ Jesus. Being present in the Lord is to have been transformed into one who searches after the thoughts of God. To be absent from the body is to have thoughts that are not carnal but thoughts that are like-minded with Jesus. A resurrection mindset brings thoughts such as doubt and lack of belief to an end in exchange for thoughts that seek to understand the one who is life.

> When Jesus heard that, He said, "This sickness is not unto death, but for the glory of God, that the Son of God may be glorified through it." Now Jesus loved Martha and her sister and Lazarus. So, when He heard that he was sick, He stayed two more days in the place where He was. Then after this He said to the disciples, "Let us go to Judea again." The disciples said to Him, "Rabbi, lately the Jews sought to stone You, and are You going there again?"
>
> —John 11:4–8

Jesus had an intimate personal relationship with Lazarus and his sisters, Mary and Martha. God allowed Lazarus to become ill and die to reveal to others that Jesus's word is so much more powerful than any living circumstance or any dead situation that confronts us. God was glorified because the end result proved that no adversities, no adversary, and neither sickness nor death can stop God's love and the power of his word. Having a relationship with Jesus similar to that of Lazarus, Mary, and Martha allows dead, embarrassing, difficult, and smelly areas in our past, present, or future to be exposed to who he is and the I Am we need him to be. Jesus took the difficult challenges this family faced and changed them into something good for them so that they could live life more abundantly in him. Trusting Jesus as one who operates the process puts to death thinking that the struggle is greater than the one who lives inside us. The struggle in living out our purpose is in the journey and the lessons learned in this process where we come to know that our life and being are in knowing who Jesus is. Those who seek purpose understand that this is the road to living life more abundantly, which in time makes the struggle worth it, in the process. Living life on purpose is what separates believers who have an abundant life from others who do not. Living life more abundantly means living life with the purpose God anointed you to have. The ultimate relationship one can have with God through Jesus is a type of death that separates people, places, and things that limit you from living life with purpose. Lazarus was the ultimate example of what it cost to be loved by Jesus and to love him. Anything that dies so that God is glorified shall live with purpose and have life more abundantly.

This is the day the Lord has made; let us rejoice and be glad in it is a faith-based prelude toward worshipping the Lord. It is declaring the end of a day before the beginning of that day based on truth and not facts that makes the process worth the struggle.

I own a MacBook Pro laptop computer, which I greatly depend on daily for writing books, paying bills, reading email, and more. When my computer stops working efficiently, I take it to the Apple store for service and not just to anyone who provides computer services. For the same reason, believers rejoice and are glad in the day the Lord has made because no one else can service and help followers to perform at their best other than the manufacturer, God. He not only created you but also knows the plans he has for you to succeed and perform effectively in your purpose.

Because God is omnipresent and omniscient, believers are empowered to declare that no matter what happens, including the facts stated throughout the day, God remains in control always. Worshipping God creates a joyful sound that proclaims, "Jehovah-jireh, I will trust the power of your ability as my daily provider." This is the day the Lord has made is living a life based on the truth concerning one's identity and not based on facts. Rejoicing and being glad is having a mindset to worship God in truth. Thank you, God, for Jesus, who is the key to who I am. The great I Am, who is God, is the "I am" in who we are and who we've been looking for as our true identity. As Jesus is the resurrection and life, so he is the resurrection of our intimate, personal relationship with God. His life is the only source that leads to our purpose and the true identity for everyone. It is through death similar to Lazarus's experience that believers are able to expose their purpose in Christ Jesus.

> *But whatever house you enter, first say, "Peace to this house." And if a son of peace is there, your peace will rest on it; if not, it will return to you. And remain in the same house, eating and drinking such things as they give, for the laborer is worthy of his wages. Do not go from house to house. Whatever city you enter, and they receive you, eat such things as are set before you. And heal the sick there, and say to them, "The kingdom of God has come near to you." But whatever city you enter, and they do not receive you, go out into its streets and say, "The very dust of your city which clings to us we wipe off against you. Nevertheless, know this that the kingdom of God has come near you." But I say to you that it will be more tolerable in that Day for Sodom than for that city.*
>
> —Luke 10:5–12

I remember growing up when people, including relatives, would make such statements as, "You are just like your daddy," or "You favor you father," or "You have your father's hair," or "You've got your father's nose." Or they might say, "You get your height from your father." As believers, we tend to look for God in others, but today I'm here to say you favor God and because you favor your Heavenly Father, the kingdom of God is much closer to you than you think. Sometimes, it becomes more challenging to see Jesus working in the current circumstance of followers, especially under unexpected adversities. When we do not see Jesus, faith takes its rightful place in directing the path to knowing who Jesus is.

> *And when the disciples saw him walking on the sea, they were troubled, saying, It is a spirit; and they cried out for fear. But straightway Jesus spake unto them, saying, Be of good cheer; it is I; be not afraid. And Peter answered him and said, Lord, if it be thou, bid me come unto thee on the water. And he said, Come. And when Peter was come down out of the ship, he walked on the water, to go to Jesus. But when he saw the wind boisterous, he was afraid; and beginning to sink, he cried, saying, Lord, save me. And immediately Jesus stretched forth his hand, and caught him, and said unto him, O thou of little faith, wherefore didst thou doubt?*
>
> —Matt. 14:26–31 KJV

Jesus's thought process is a mindset that God advised people to have. It is this type of thought process where people can find rest in the midst of any distractions from discovering their true identity in him. God used the experience on the water to teach Peter that God is the same Lord that allowed him to walk on the water and is the same Lord when he caught him from sinking in the water. Jesus wants everyone to see him as faith and the substance that can change our outlook in seeing who he is in every experience, good or bad. It is in the struggles we have in trusting God that Jesus is asking at what point in this journey you stopped believing that I Am has always been there for you. Subsequently, it's always in the struggle that we come to know that he has never left, and because of this, the struggles are worth going through.

It's nice to see God in others and see him working in our struggling situations. In this is the day the Lord has made, he put in people a part of who he is and gave people the free will to choose to discover what he already did and what plans he has already chosen for them to succeed. God has already given people the victory simply when he decreed. Let us rejoice and be glad in this day as chosen vessels for purpose from a God who is the source of every resource.

Faith, like God, is a source that creates resources that work to produce an effective outcome. For example, if your heart desires to eat at a seafood restaurant, God will give you the necessary resources to work that desire into fruition along with whatever things are needed to eat there. God will not deliver the seafood restaurant to your doorstep though he has the power to do so. God created people in his likeness and image to demonstrate the creativity with the resources he gives to people. Although God blesses you, you are required to work the resources to produce the final outcome.

Worth the Struggle is a personal journey to discover the truth of who you are and to live as it relates to purpose, which is your true identity. The journey helps to develop the type of faith needed in the transformation process between the old understanding of who you are and a new way of understanding as a born-again believer. This journey of being born again is a return flight to the place where God spoke your purpose into existence before you were conceived in your mother's womb. To be born again is to return to the state of mind in God where the revelation of who you are in his thoughts becomes your new reality. The revelations of who you are as it relates to purpose are found in the kingdom of God. However, it is not accessible in our old way of thinking but only by having a mindset like Jesus and through the power of his spirit. Believing that you have been created by God for a purpose is the born-again experience, which requires faith for it to work. Knowing that you are born again is similar to how the wind operates; it is something that you cannot see with your natural eye, but there's something within you that pushes you into destiny. The Holy Spirit empowers born-again people to fulfill their purpose and gives them the power to do everything that God has called them to do. Born-again people will have others feeling puzzled about where the source of this power is coming from simply because it is by his spirit and not a person.

> *There was a man of the Pharisees named Nicodemus, a ruler of the Jews. This man came to Jesus by night and said to Him, "Rabbi, we know that You are a teacher come from God; for no one can do these signs that You do unless God is with him." Jesus answered and said to him, "Most assuredly, I say to you, unless one is born again, he cannot see the kingdom of God." Nicodemus said to Him, "How can a man be born when he is old? Can he enter a second time into his mother's womb and be born?" Jesus answered, "Most assuredly, I say to you, unless one is born of water and the Spirit, he cannot enter the kingdom of God. That which is born of the flesh is flesh, and that which is born of the Spirit is spirit. Do not marvel that I said to you, 'You must be born again.' The wind blows where it wishes, and you hear the sound of it, but cannot tell where it comes from and where it goes. So is everyone who is born of the Spirit."*
>
> —John 3:1–9

SPIRITUAL DARKROOMS IN THE STRUGGLE

CHAPTER 7

A Spiritual darkroom in the struggle is a mindset that is developed from life lessons learned along the way in the pursuit of purpose. It is the thought process where faith becomes the only true source of getting you to the kingdom of God to understand your purpose. He will use struggles to expose a believer's gifts in preparation for purpose; however, faith becomes the substance for believers who are called according to his purpose. Spiritual darkrooms are experiences in the life of believers where weeping may endure throughout the night, but joy comes quickly in the morning. Seeking first the kingdom of God is the true route toward discovering the place in your mind where God lives, moves, and has his being. Believers are transformed in this renewed mind of thinking like Jesus. The kingdom of God becomes accessible for people on earth to enter into his presence. The transformation process prepares people for change to take place in the born-again experience. Believers must have a mindset like that of Jesus to see spiritual darkrooms as places where God does his best work creating and developing gifts to work with the purpose in the life of the believer prior to being exposed to the light. The light, in this case, is the understanding of the truth of who you are according to the purpose that God created you for. "For we walk by faith, not by sight" (2 Corinthians 5:7). A spiritual darkroom is a state of mind where true worshippers rejoice and are glad because they know and trust God, who controls all things. It is in this process that Jesus becomes the new way of thinking and where people learn to adjust their new perception of thinking, facilitating transformation and change. The challenge in transiting from transformation to change is when there are no prior thoughts of conviction or belief in wanting to change. It is not until there is a conviction to believe that the struggle in the process of God's plan is worth the work by changing the way you think. "Being confident of this very thing, that he which hath begun a good work in you will perform it until the day of Jesus Christ" (Philippians 1:6 KJV).

Usually top-shelf merchandise is considered the best a merchant has to offer. God often hides and places the believer's gift on the top shelf of living life with purpose. This will often cause the believer to stretch toward the gift that God has placed inside the believer starting from ground zero. The top shelf is a different mindset that is above a follower's old way of thinking. Anyone who has been transformed from their old thought process becomes more effective when living life with purpose. The challenge for some believers is understanding that gifts from God and purpose must collaborate. This collaboration of the anointing and the appointed time is similar to the collaboration of faith and works. When collaboration fails to take place between the gift and working with purpose, people may feel a sense of struggle of not knowing how to function effectively in their gift. Reaching and stretching toward destiny helps transform the old perception from the formal way of thinking into the new perception of thinking. Having the same mindset of Jesus is the glue that holds faith and works together; consequently, it's this same bond that helps keep people perfectly aligned with their anointing and the appointed time. Faith, at times, like an employer, will say, "I am waiting for you to start the orientation process." Some people look at faith similar to new employees who may wonder how the orientation process is going to turn out, but at the same time, they have not lost hope in the process. Faith requires people like an employer to work the word even when the end product can't be seen. Revelation by God gives clarity in the process, which helps make the struggle worth it to those who are living in the purpose of their gift. This new perception offers followers a better understanding of the substance of what faith is and a better understanding of who Jesus is as the author and finisher of our faith. Faith is to the anointing as work is to the appointed time. The gift or the anointing within is activated by faith; however, for it to function effectively, the appointed time becomes the workplace for the gift to work. To do this, a believer must understand the substance of faith. Without faith, it is impossible to please God. Delight yourself in the Lord, and he will give you the desires of your heart. The desire of a believer's heart is to please God. To please God, people must invest themselves in a personal, intimate relationship with Jesus. Sometimes, the work required from individuals to move a mountain is simply believing in who Jesus is. One of the amazing things about believing in Jesus is that he is so faithful regardless whether our measure of faith is small or large. I believe God wants people to work smarter and not harder by simply believing in him as the substance of faith, knowing he is omniscient. Changing the way we think to thinking like Jesus, changes the old thought process into seeing things the way he does. In other words, God is so big in faith that all we need is a little faith, and then we can go big in believing, and it will be more than enough.

> *Jesus said to him, "If you can believe, all things are possible to him who believes." Immediately the father of the child cried out and said with tears, "Lord, I believe; help my unbelief!" When Jesus saw that the people came running together, He rebuked the unclean spirit, saying to it, "Deaf and dumb spirit, I command you, come out of him and enter him no more!"*
>
> —Mark 9:23–25

This is where the impossible becomes possible in pleasing God. Jesus seeks people interested in the substance of who he is in their mission, not in knowing him because of his position.

In developing pictures, water is used to remove harmful chemicals as the final step in a darkroom. The same is true in spiritual darkrooms; however, water in this case comes from the Holy Spirit flowing into the hearts of followers, causing them to believe as the Scripture has said concerning who Jesus is. Because faith operates best in dark conditions, believers must trust the operating system or process that faith collaborates best with work. "Through faith we understand that the worlds were framed by the word of God, so that things which are seen were not made of things which do appear" (Hebrews 11:3 KJV). The chemicals used in a darkroom for developing pictures are harmful yet necessary in developing negatives into photographs. Spiritual darkrooms, or the steps that God has ordered, are used to frame a believer's true identity. Although at times they can be harmful, they still are necessary for fruition in spite of any struggle a person may face in this process.

This is the day the Lord has made can be viewed as a spiritual darkroom filled with dangerous chemicals that have the potential to harm, but because God is faithful, no weapons or chemicals formed against believers will prosper. Just being in a darkroom can be frightening and dangerous, especially if you are clueless about how to maneuver in unfamiliar places. A spiritual darkroom is a type of mindset for individuals to use faith as a guide to living, moving, and functioning effectively in search of their true identity in God. Faith does its best work as a guide for believers in spiritually dark places. When David walked in the shadows of death, he feared no evil because God's rod and staff comforted him. This thinking empowered him to understand why spiritual darkrooms were designed to further his development for a specific purpose. "This is the day the Lord has made; let us rejoice and be glad in it" was never about what type of day followers were to experience, but rather a call to acknowledge the one who created the day. Consequently, the day is not about what you got out of it, but a consistent form of worship to the one who made the day. As a result, rejoicing and being glad becomes a by-product of a personal relationship with the one who created the day in spite of the type of day one is having.

An example of being a true worshipper is having the mental capacity to catch what appears to be a negative life experience as an opportunity for seeing who God is. The question is not what kind of day you are having, but knowing I Am is in your day, be it good, bad, or indifferent with or without struggles.

> *For scarcely for a righteous man will one die; yet perhaps for a good man someone would even dare to die. But God demonstrates His own love toward us, in that while we were still sinners, Christ died for us. Much more then, having now been justified by His blood, we shall be saved from wrath through Him.*
>
> —Rom. 5:7–9

As believers, we rejoice and are glad in the day the Lord has made in spite of spiritual darkrooms simply because of God's commitment to the substance of who Jesus is (faith). Faith is where our purpose is promised to come to fruition while we experience spiritual darkrooms. In these spiritual darkrooms, God exposes purpose in man, facilitated by his faithfulness and directed to further destiny. Nazareth, where Jesus was raised as a child, was known as a very wicked place for its obscure lifestyle. In addition, it was despised and looked down upon by other nearby cities. Even the people of Galilee felt it was a miserable place to live. How could anything good come from there? "And Nathanael said to him, 'Can anything good come out of Nazareth?' Philip said to him, 'Come and see'" (John 1:46).

It's a question a believer might have: Can anything good come from a negative while in a darkroom? Why is a photograph—the end product—more sought after than the negative? Although the negative may be looked upon as an unfinished product, God looks at negatives always as their value in the future, and he holds a high regard for the process the negative goes through to reach its final outcome. He sees the finished product while it is still in its negative state, and he speaks to the negative as though it has reached its purpose. This is done simply because his faith overrides anything that has not yet appeared. In photography, negatives are required to re-create and enlarge the image of an object. God creates a believer's true identity and captures it on a negative. However, God does not intend for the believer's purpose to stay in the form of a negative. It must go through the process to fruition. Nazareth, the place where God selected for Jesus to grow up as a child, was known only for its meanness, weakness, and obscurity; yet God saw good in the form of purpose in a most negative environment. It wasn't until the purpose of Jesus became fully developed in the eyes of others that they were able to see a much better picture of the son of God, who came from Nazareth. In many cases, a negative or undeveloped purpose from God can be viewed as a paradox in which viewers' first perception is not always what the creator intended and a second look helps viewers see something quite different from what they saw at first. "And we know that all things work together for good to those who love God, to those who are the called according to His purpose" (Romans 8:28).

God's faithfulness will ensure his promise concerning the purpose for man regardless of whether the environment or circumstance surrounding the purpose is wicked, mean, or obscure. "And the LORD said to Satan, 'Behold, all that he has is in your power; only do not lay a hand on his person'" (Job 1:12). In spite of what a believer faces in any given day, faith should be placed in God's intentional plans for negatives and the purpose he has placed in every negative. There is a warranty on the anointed even when purpose is in the negative state and before its appointed time. This warranty comes from God's love for the world and for those who remain a work in progress in discovering their purpose through him. God's faithfulness doesn't expire, and there is no shelf life regardless of how many ordered steps individuals must take to reach their true identity. Jesus's response to Peter's ups and downs while walking on water was a great demonstration of God's faithfulness and grace. This gift provides believers the encouragement needed in moments of falling short or falling down or feeling unable to measure up to God's expectations.

In God's plan, pain is often needed in a spiritual darkroom to push people into living their purpose. Rest has a unique function in the birthing process of purpose. The pain from contractions and the natural birthing process is used as a sign that it's time to push. The pushing doesn't cause the painful muscle contractions. The pain works in collaboration with the mother's pushing. After each contraction and before the next contraction, the woman is strongly encouraged to rest, but it is not a type of rest that promotes sleep. It's a time to gather her strength, her confidence, and her focus for the next push. Rest periods in the spiritual darkroom work similarly. During rest in the spiritual darkroom, people become empowered for the next step toward their destiny in the day-of process.

The pain makes the struggle real for expectant believers and is necessary for destiny to be delivered. Pain and pleasure are opposites in life; yet they are often paired together in a spiritual darkroom to illustrate how the power of God becomes pleasure to people in painful times. Giving birth to destiny is both painful and most pleasurable. Women were created to give life; yet not all are chosen or choose to bear children. However, in other areas in their lives, they bring life to fruition.

The discomfort of giving birth to life or to destiny, can make people feel as though they are in a spiritual darkroom. The spiritual darkroom is where purpose is born, and it is this process where faith in Jesus as the author and finisher of your destiny becomes the new normal in understanding how God sees you in purpose form. This is where the word of God speaks life and illuminates his son as a light over what he has created by faith. A spiritual darkroom or feeling challenged with adversities helps you discover who you are in Jesus. These moments can be oppositional yet also be seen as opportunities; this is another example of the paradox concept. Seeing the birthing process of purpose the way God does empowers people to cope effectively with pain and pleasure in achieving their purpose. Finding the rhythm between resting and being pushed to your destiny can be challenging. The resting place in between pushing and destiny is that place of regrouping before the next contraction or adversity. A spiritual darkroom is not the place of destiny, even though it gives birth to purpose. It's a starting place for people to walk out and work out what they were created to do.

As an acute psychiatric nurse in an inpatient unit, I facilitated support groups to enable patients to improve effective coping skills many times by changing the way they processed information. When I earned my doctorate in nursing, I just assumed that God was going to raise me to the next level of responsibility by blessing me with a leadership and management position. Although I applied for various opportunities, a promotion did not happen, and I remained as a floor nurse on an acute mental health locked unit and continued delivering care and optimal services to patients.

After 12 years as a floor nurse, five of which I had a doctoral degree in nursing, I started seeing the place where I worked as a labor room of my destiny. That happened once I began to worship God as a strategic planner. God revealed that where I was working and my level of function were not my destiny, but it was being used as a spiritual darkroom in preparation for my destiny. I felt the pain and discomfort of knowing that the spiritual darkroom was not my place of purpose but a place of preparation for my destiny. I felt the pain and disappointment in not yet reaching my appointed time and tried to learn how best to use where I was and what I was. I had to learn to see myself as a floor nurse who already was the leader and change agent that God saw in me without the stage, the lights, the crowds, and all the benefits that come with the appointed time. Once I got this in my spirit and my thoughts, I used the small support groups that I facilitated on my unit as though as I was speaking to thousands of people seeking to know who God is.

After David was anointed king of Israel, he quickly returned to keeping the sheep. Similarly, God chose to send me back to tend his sheep as a floor nurse with a doctorate in nursing to care for mentally challenged patients. If truth be told, I am embarrassed that it took me so long to see what God was seeing and the plan that he had for me before my mother ever met my father. God saw me as anointed with an appointed time.

One of the most important and vital parts of human life is the mind. God trusted and chose me as his daughter to help treat the minds of patients who suffer from mental illness in addition to people who do not realize the importance and power behind how they think. A person's body, behaviors, and life-changing choices often follow how and what a person thinks. With this in mind, God shared with believers to let that same mind that's in Christ Jesus be in them. Keep your mindset on the teachings of Jesus and the substance of who he is. Do not allow what appears in the natural to be a temporary emotional setback to dictate to your destiny. That can foster feelings of insecurity.

For years, I have been rushing to get away from working as a floor nurse in mental health. At the same time, God was increasing my territory in the spiritual darkroom while using my position as a floor nurse. Lesson learned. Do not view the years spent caring for sheep as a shepherd as lost time or waiting for God for deliverance while in what appears to be a spiritual darkroom. I used the dayroom at work where I taught support groups as a platform to prepare myself for the next stage. I became excited over the small gatherings of patients with mental health challenges and saw them as a ministry in preparation for speaking to thousands of people seeking to know God while broken, disgusted, and confused. God instructs followers to "despise not the day of small beginnings."

> *You have heard that it was said, "Love your neighbor and hate your enemy." But I tell you, love your enemies and pray for those who persecute you, that you may be children of your Father in heaven. He causes his sun to rise on the evil and the good and sends rain on the righteous and the unrighteous. If you love those who love you, what reward will you get? Are not even the tax collectors doing that? And if you greet only your own people, what are you doing more than others? Do not even pagans do that? Be perfect, therefore, as your heavenly Father is perfect.*
>
> —Matthew 5:43–48 NIV

God controls everything, even the adversary and adversities as well as the steps to reach destiny. Pray for your enemies because God often uses them to push you to your destiny. The enemy is not sent to kill you but to assist in your preparation for destiny—sometimes as a tool to cut and shape you into your purpose. God will allow enemies to cut you, and as a result, you may feel pain and discomfort, but he is aware of what you are feeling and your struggles. However, at the same time, his focus is on the mission of preparing you for purpose and for the father's glory, which makes the struggle worth going through. God is love, and love is merciful; nevertheless, he is purpose-driven. He is purpose-driven. The transition stage from the cut to glory is a time for healing after the cutting and reshaping in which change takes its rightful place. Because God is faithful, his grace is more than sufficient in every struggle.

GOD IS FAITHFUL IN
THE STRUGGLE

CHAPTER 8

"They are new every morning; Great is Your faithfulness. 'The Lord is my portion,' says my soul, 'Therefore I hope in Him!' The LORD is good to those who wait for Him, to the soul who seeks Him" (Lamentations 3:23–25). Finding the real you in pursuing your destiny is a faith journey. Faith becomes more developed in learning about the great faithfulness of God in the struggle. This development of faith often comes when followers are challenged in the struggle while discovering their true identity. God's faithfulness becomes more evident for believers who go through the process of living life in the purpose he created them to live in.

"Before I formed you in the womb I knew you, before you were born I set you apart; I appointed you as a prophet to the nations" (Jeremiah 1:5 NIV). There is a profound connection between his rest and his great faithfulness. God finds rest in his faithfulness. By his faith, all creations were manifested. His rest is not in the finished product but in his faith. God's word is faith, and because he believes and is faithful to his word, he finds rest in it. God's rest is not like how people rest, such as taking a relaxing break from working. On the contrary, God finds rest in the work supported by faith. "And we know that all things work together for good to those who love God, to those who are the called according to His purpose" (Romans 8:28). This scripture shares how God wants others to find rest and comfort in his word by faith.

God's rest is the end result of his faithfulness and those who worship him as God. The season of rest for God takes place where seeds of purpose are planted in fertilized soil and nourished by the substance of faith. Here, the work by believers is animated by who he is and not the productivity of the seeds. Servants or believers who are in the presence of God when he is at rest are true worshippers. God finds rest when believers worship him by acknowledging who he is, regardless of whether anointed believers have reached their appointed time.

The most challenging steps God orders for his anointed believers are the steps just before the appointed time. It can be very challenging and at times a struggle to understand or appreciate the challenging steps between the time of the anointing and the appointed time, in which faith is now a required component. Often, this lack of understanding increases levels of anxiety. Believers must trust in God that rivers of living waters will flow, even if reality reminds them that they are in a desert with no evidence of water present. "Let God be true but every man a liar" (Romans 3:4). When God first thinks of his word, it becomes whatever he speaks into existence. Because God is not a man, he cannot lie. He can rest in the word that he speaks. God wants his followers to find rest in his faithfulness. "God having provided something better for us, that they should not be made perfect apart from us" (Hebrews 11:40). God knew his children before they were formed in their mother's womb and before they were ordained, and he anointed them before they performed or walked in their calling, gifts, or purpose. After we are born, we become doers of what God has already known us to be. God's great faithfulness is revealed to followers in the process of exposing their true identity. The conversation that God had with Jesus and the Holy Spirit concerning your true identity and purpose becomes accessible in seeking the kingdom of heaven. Many times, God will use adversities in the process to help followers be exposed to their true identity. In every believer lies a purpose, which is a type of Superman kept under cover like Clark Kent. When God exposes who we are in him during the transformation process, believers see him as faithful.

"Then God blessed the seventh day and sanctified it, because in it He rested from all His work which God had created and made" (Genesis 2:3). God believed so much in his word, which created the world and all its creations, that he found a resting place. In his presence, God exposes followers to their callings and destiny and, soon, to their appointed time. Moreover, in the presence of the Lord, there is a resting place where his word (Jesus) becomes the resurrection and the life for individuals looking to be restored or born again. Anyone who believes with his or her heart and confesses with his or her mouth that Jesus is Lord will have everlasting life. God finds rest knowing that eternal life is available for people who seek a personal relationship with Jesus. There is a state of rest for God in his word, which prompts him to be faithful to his word (Jesus). *Worth the Struggle* is clearly about a journey in this is the day the Lord has made that prepares people to rest in his word and to be glad and rejoice in it. People who have a personal yet intimate relationship with Jesus have a resting place in God while in the middle of a storm. Because he is faithful to his word (Jesus), the commitment that God has with his son keeps a resting place accessible for others to believe that he is who he said he is. God's word is his bond, and his bond, which is Jesus, is the glue that sticks people to who God is. Walking in Jesus rather than beside him means knowing the substance of who Jesus is through a personal relationship and not the limited version of man's perception of who he is. "God is a Spirit: and they that worship him must worship him in spirit and in truth" (John 4:24 KJV).

Out of the belly of believers, God by the power of the Holy Spirit, brings revelation to callings and fruition to purpose that makes the struggle worth pursuing. Believers who perform the necessary work as doers of the word demonstrate faith in who God is, which enhances the manifestation for his glory. Followers must believe that his word is who he said he is, and his word will never return to him as insufficient funds. Because God is faithful, there remains a rest for the people of God: "For he who has entered His rest has himself also ceased from his works as

God did from His" (Hebrews 4:10). Faith is to work as hope is to the ability to rest in the relationship with God through Jesus in spite of any circumstances contrary to our destiny. God is a promise keeper and he is going to do what he says he is going to do. A rest period always follows a time of God's great faithfulness.

God's great faithfulness led to Jesus being found resting in the belly of a boat during an unexpected and strange storm, which caused the men traveling with Jesus to question Jesus's concern for their safety. God wants us to learn from Jesus, with the power of the Holy Spirit, to find rest in the unexpected and strange storms that come into life, rather than allowing in anxiety, fear, and doubts about who God is. God promises rest for followers facing adversity. God uses struggles such as adversities in the lives of believers for them to find encouragement that can only be found in a state of rest while in the presence of God. Struggles that show up in periods of confusion and discomfort often bring to the surface signs of weakness; however, believers are made strong in these times of weakness through Jesus. Moreover, individuals will come to understand this concept better in the process of living life with purpose.

> *And He said to me, "My grace is sufficient for you, for My strength is made perfect in weakness." Therefore, most gladly I will rather boast in my infirmities, that the power of Christ may rest upon me. Therefore, I take pleasure in infirmities, in reproaches, in needs, in persecutions, in distresses, for Christ's sake. For when I am weak, then I am strong.*
>
> —2 Cor. 12:9–10

Struggles are sometimes sent by God to break through whatever is keeping followers from knowing how to rest in him when coping with challenges. Our greatness is in God's great faithfulness; however, his faithfulness is not revealed to believers until they can believe that God is resting in what he has already given us to possess. Very often, God will reveal the end of his promise and then rest in the power of his word while we are going through the process of reaching toward the end.

Adversities promote and foster tenancy in the process that motivates people in reaching the promised gift. God is resting in the process and not at the end of what he had promised. Resting in his perfect peace when faced with adversity is a type of worship. This acknowledgment tells others who God is and how his word relates to his promises during the process and difficult times.

When I bought my current home, I created a separate room for God to rest in. It was an extended built-in office space in the master bedroom. This extension in my room was where I retreated after a difficult day at work and at times while caring for Jerry. It was also a place where I had made poor choices including sleeping with men to whom I was not married. Initially, I felt indifferent about creating a space for God to rest while my life mirrored a construction site for purpose. Because God is faithful, his love and grace allow him to find rest in the chaos when people are in the process of discovering their purpose. I am so amazed at how God evaluates a construction site where purpose is being developed. He overlooks the mess and never loses sight of what he promises. Before the day of ground-breaking for purpose, God speaks his word. God is so faithful to his word that he is the only true example of what it's like to believe in something in spite of what it looks like in the process and before the manifestation. Because God is so faithful, he can find rest in a mess. His faith empowers him to rest. God instructs people in his word how to find rest in a mess by the way of what influences the way they think. "Let this mind be in you which was also in Christ Jesus" (Philippians 2:5). This thought process that God wants people to have in Jesus provides perfect peace even in the midst of a mess. "You will keep him in perfect peace, whose mind is stayed on You, because he trusts in You" (Isaiah 26:3).

Until believers see adversity as a tool to get them to the promise, adversity will be viewed as a never-ending struggle or a distraction to prevent them from seeing the truth. Distractions in the process are often used to empower people to dig deeper by looking beyond the adversity and seeing Jesus as the greater one who lives within them. The mess at a construction site can distract individuals from seeing the purpose of what is being built. The journey into his presence is where challenges are perceived as lessons to assist individuals in developing a more intimate relationship with God through Jesus. These lessons support the transformation process of becoming the real you, which is a by-product of God's great faithfulness. Adversities are tools propelling people toward their destiny as they strive toward knowing who God is in the process.

God is the best version of who you are because he knows the plans that he has for everything he created. Gas in a car serves to transport the car from one place to another. Faith, as it relates to the process of seeking the kingdom of God, works to transport the believer to the presence of Jesus in hopes of discovering the believer's true identity and purpose. In worship, hope is the result of faith. Moreover, the association of hope and worship are as essential as water is to life. Hope in worship acknowledges who God is without having to be physically connected to who God is. "God is Spirit, and those who worship Him must worship in spirit and truth" (John 4:24). In his presence, we discover hope, and the substance of that faith is through Jesus. Often in the struggle, there are moments in the process where we strive for or toward purpose, which in many cases fosters anxiety. However, it is in the struggle and the feelings of anxiety that we, as followers, understand that the ground we stand on is holy, and faith becomes the substance that the ground is made of. God's faithfulness is evident in his omnipresence. So instead of looking for faith or waiting for faith, just believe that God's faithfulness is the ground that empowers people to stand.

The woman with the issue of blood for 12 years was in the presence of God and was empowered to believe in who he is. Because she was standing in his presence, she just needed to touch the hem of his garment to become well. "But without faith it is impossible to please Him, for he who comes to God must believe that He is, and that He is a rewarder of those who diligently seek Him" (Hebrews 11:6). The woman with the issue of blood for 12 years understood that the ground she was standing on was holy because she came into his presence in the faith of who Jesus is.

Then He said, "Do not draw near this place. Take your sandals off your feet, for the place where you stand is holy ground." Moreover He said, "I am the God of your father—the God of Abraham, the God of Isaac, and the God of Jacob." And Moses hid his face, for he was afraid to look upon God.

—Exod. 3:5–6

To be in the presence of God is to be perfectly aligned with Jesus. At this point, you can ask anything in his name, and he will grant it to you: "And I will do whatever you ask in my name, so that the Father may be glorified in the Son." (John 14:13 NIV).

"Looking unto Jesus, the author and finisher of our faith" (Hebrews 12:2). This connection between being in the presence of God, standing on holy ground, and knowing that substance of the ground is composed of who Jesus is through the power of the Holy Spirit brings us in a complete circle, which in essence gives rise to our destiny. This is the place where God is no longer a mystery but a reality, as is written in Matthew 6:33 (NIV): "Seek first his kingdom and his righteousness, and all these things will be given to you as well." The place where God rests is where faith is expected to go into action.

In the parable of the tares and the wheat, the field illustrates the day God has made. Although the wheat was surrounded with weeds, the unexpected adversary, the wheat still holds promise to reach its purpose because of God's faithfulness. Rejoicing and being glad should not be limited to an emotional response to who God is or what he has done, but rather it stems from true worshippers understanding the substance by which faith comes. They know how to work the measure of faith they were given by God. "As God has dealt to each one a measure of faith" (Romans 12:3). God looks for each measure of faith given to people and its application in the day he has made. The application of faith moves believers to a state of rejoicing and being glad because their mindset is toward seeking the one who made the day and is not stuck on the challenges that came with the day.

"Another parable He spoke to them: 'The kingdom of heaven is like leaven, which a woman took and hid in three measures of meal till it was all leavened'" (Matthew 13:33). When believers apply their work to the faith in who Jesus is, there is a point of rest. Knowing who Jesus is as the substance in faith is like understanding the power of yeast when applied to dough in preparation for baking bread: there is a point of rest where the dough is set aside for the yeast to work and rise. Faith is not only a living substance, but it was created to work in collaboration among believers to please God. "But without faith it is impossible to please him: for he that cometh to God must believe that he is, and that he is a rewarder of them that diligently seek him" (Hebrews 11:6 KJV). People can find rest in God's presence by pleasing him. The challenge for some is that having the understanding, faith, and pleasing God often cause one to have conflicting feelings or emotions. Faith operates out of a source where hope is the only evidence available when faced with adversity. In this case, learning to work smarter and not harder will empower people to see through this thought process that rest and pleasing God often bring adversities and adversary. When this takes place, it becomes an opportunity for God to show up and show out on your behalf. Perhaps our prayer as a people should be, "Lord, give us the understanding of the work that would lead to a type of rest necessary to develop the faith you already placed, rather than asking to increase the faith."

The challenge for most followers is how to work the measure of substance of the faith that God gave them initially. Like making pie crust, there is a certain method of work to get the result we seek. Like pie dough, the substance of faith requires individuals to knead the dough using the strength of their hands and arm muscles. Making more dough won't make the crust flaky; however, working the dough in the right method does. In the day-of process, people discover their purpose in the substance of faith or the core of who Jesus is. In this is the day that the Lord has made, which empowers others to discover their destiny in spite of challenges faced along the way. God sees these same barriers as opportunities for followers to believe in him and his faithfulness as a way of bringing them to their destiny. The challenge for so many people is getting to the place of believing before they have developed into their purpose. Yet faith empowers people to see beyond the kneading to the hope of the finished crust through a new way of seeing. Too often, followers seek ways to increase their level of faith without realizing that the amount they have is sufficient. However, the challenge could be not knowing how to work with what they have. Similarly, there is an art to making homemade whipped cream. If you overbeat the heavy cream, it will turn to butter. People are given all the essential tools and the right measures concerning faith to do the purpose God has given them. As followers continue to grow and develop their ability to work the measure of faith that God has already placed in them, the understanding of their true identity in God's plans for success becomes clearer. Both heavy cream and pie dough have to be worked before the end product and before reaching their purpose. However, too much work will keep the dough from being a flaky pie crust and over-whipping the cream will turn it into a solid mass. When work becomes the focal point, it makes faith limited in what it was created to do, and as a result, the outcome is less desirable. The true understanding of faith is knowing the core of who Jesus is. The quality of the day does not cause true worshippers to rejoice and be glad; however, it is the substance of who Jesus is that allows them to acknowledge what is truth in spite of adversities. Faith is a living substance, not a concept or a great idea.

In the last several weeks of caring for Jerry, he became more dependent for assistance with daily living needs and felt greater uncertainty about how this was going to end with no cure in sight. At that moment in Jerry's journey, I realized that the best way to help him was to be his spiritual midwife. To me, Jerry's biggest challenge was not in finding comfort in his fight with ALS but in finding comfort or rest in his journey of knowing that God is faithful in this is the day that the Lord has made. God will often illustrate his promises by the way of presenting problems. God led me from being Jerry's wife for over 10 years to being his ex-wife, to being his caregiver and midwife. As his midwife, I was assigned to help Jerry see God's faithfulness in times of discomfort and uncertainty in his journey with ALS. The promise was that Jerry would come to the feet of Jesus. I shared with Jerry that we needed to place our focus less on the things we could not change, like the disease process, and more on the promised land. I prompted Jerry to look toward worship, seeing God's promises and his faithfulness as an alternative way of seeing the disease process. Jerry's response was, "Althea, would you worship with me?" I held Jerry's hand, and we worshipped together. I called God by his numerous names and words that best describe who God is. We acknowledged who God was in Jerry's journey while coping with ALS. After Jerry and I worshipped, his physical discomforts from ALS did not decrease or leave. However, it was no longer a distraction keeping us from seeing God as being faithful in the day of process. I saw how God used Jerry's uncertainty and discomfort to give me purpose as a midwife. I took every opportunity with Jerry to encourage him to sit at the feet of Jesus through worship during his last days on earth. Soothing Jerry's discomfort and uncertainty about how his journey with ALS was going to end became my purpose as his midwife. I believe I was led by the Holy Spirit to bring Jerry to the feet of Jesus when discomfort and uncertainty became increasingly more distracting to him than seeing God for who he is as faithful in this is the day that the Lord has made.

The Bible includes a story in Luke 10:39–42 where Mary sat at the feet of Jesus while her sister worked in the kitchen and complained about Mary not being available to help her with the housework. Martha chose to work in the kitchen, versus Mary, who sat at the feet of her faith to hear and receive what Jesus had to say. Jesus's response to Martha's complaints was to enlighten Martha about things that are life-changing rather than the things we change that have only a temporary effect on life. Revelation is what moved Mary to know who Jesus is as the source of her faith. By hearing his words, she received the faith. Transitioning from Jerry's ex-wife to care provider to midwife during his dying process empowered me to use the measure of faith given to me by God to see Jerry transition from illness to living a healthier eternal life in the presence of God. My transition from caregiver to midwife placed me in a position where faith became my source of operation in providing care for Jerry, not just his physical needs. I had to believe that God would provide Jerry the spiritual things he needed while in transition. I had to believe that Jerry's illness served a purpose even in his pain, discomfort, and uncertainty. I believe hours, maybe minutes, before Jerry left to be with the Lord, he placed his belief more on who God is than the disease process of ALS. I believe he finally stopped looking at the struggle he had with discomfort and uncertainties of the disease process and began to work on trusting in who God is. Could it be that the struggle and the hardest part of the work as it relates to faith is not the physical work but understanding the substance and the application of faith within ourselves? Jerry demonstrated the hard work necessary when living with ALS; however, there comes a point where faith must do its perfect work, and we must rest in knowing that God is faithful. "Knowing that the testing of your faith produces patience. But let patience have its perfect work, that you may be perfect and complete, lacking nothing" (James 1:2–4).

Worth the Struggle as it relates to tapping into one's purpose could be perceived as working through daily challenges through life experiences in this is the day that the Lord has made. However, the struggle becomes worth it as individuals get to know better who God is in the process and know him as the one who is the process. The struggle in, some cases, for followers is the testing of their faith in the process. Yet this is the place where God is most glorified; nevertheless, without faith, it is impossible to please him. People who are learning to live life with purpose often face struggles. The struggles are used to know God as I Am in the transformation process. It is in the transformation process where people see themselves as weak or not having what it takes to facilitate the change needed to live life with purpose:

> *Then Mary said to the angel, "How can this be, since I do not know a man?" And the angel answered and said to her, "The Holy Spirit will come upon you, and the power of the Highest will overshadow you; therefore, also, that Holy One who is to be born will be called the Son of God.*
>
> —Luke 1:34–35

God is strongest in our weakest moments including any doubts and fears when we face struggles in the process. Letting patience have its perfect work is having a mindset that sees struggles as part of the process and not as adversities in the process. There are opportunities where fears and doubts can position individuals to see God as faithful in spite of a lack of faith. "Jesus said to him, 'Thomas, because you have seen Me, you have believed. Blessed are those who have not seen and yet have believed'" (John 20:29).

In the transformation process, there is a season when the anointing has not reached its appointed time. Within this time frame, I spent most of that season feeling anxious about the struggles I faced in the transformation process. I didn't always know that struggles were the lessons I needed to learn to help me to reach my destiny. I often found God resting in who he is rather than him fighting to keep struggles out of my way as I was reaching my destiny. My biggest struggle was my thought process in understanding how God can find rest in who he is while I still had to deal with the struggles of going through the transformation process. At that time, I felt and believed my struggles were bigger than who God was in my thought process versus who he is as I Am in the process. At one point, the followers in the boat with Jesus during a storm believed that their biggest struggle was the storm raging outside the boat. It wasn't until they woke up Jesus from a state of rest during the storm that their biggest struggle was not knowing the Jesus who can sleep through struggles. In the struggles, people learn to know Jesus as the prince of peace. "Ye are of God, little children, and have overcome them: because greater is he that is in you, than he that is in the world" (1 John 4:4 KJV). There are days and moments when pressing through is a struggle, but God's presence offers perfect peace, faith, grace, mercy, resurrection, life, joy, love, and so much more to those who believe that he is I Am. In fact, faith looks and waits for people who are willing to work to live their purpose. Whereas, grace and mercy seek the weak and least deserving, love finds no excuse to give of itself; life gives birth from nothing, and the resurrection restores those things that were dead. All this and more are the many reasons we should rejoice and be glad knowing that it was worth the struggle going through the process to live life on purpose. Understanding "this is the day that the Lord has made" is the key that opens the door in seeking first the kingdom of God and its righteousness. It is the place where God's thoughts of creation are revealed in a controlled environment, and his word is the protective shield over its purpose.

God will place his followers in a controlled environment to grasp the substance of who he is. Understanding by revelation is the core of who God is; this insight makes a huge difference in the lives of those who seek his presence. One of the most challenging and uncomfortable parts of the process is the decreasing of self to make room to receive the substance of who Jesus is. Jesus is the one who holds our true identity or purpose. However, the challenge or struggle doesn't limit itself here in the transformation process. The process continues as individuals transition into the change of living their life with purpose. This change empowers people to live life with purpose; it is this very change that allows people to have life more abundantly in their born-again experience. Mary was informed by the Holy Spirit that she was chosen as the blessed one among women to be pregnant and to be the mother of Jesus as her divine purpose. However, her initial reaction was to ask how this could be because she was not connected with anyone, and she didn't know anyone who could do what God had chosen her to do. "Then Mary said to the angel, 'How can this be, since I do not know a man?'" (Luke 1:34). "The sick man answered Him, 'Sir, I have no man to put me into the pool when the water is stirred up; but while I am coming, another steps down before me'" (John 5:7). There are moments in transition toward change when individuals may have to take a leap of faith to press into what God can do regardless of their natural limitations. In spite of having questions concerning how change is going to take place, some people may have a struggle with trying to see and understand with their natural eye how this is going to work out. How do you work in the struggle when things around you oppose what God is doing? In this process of transformation, for every five questions I had for God, he had only one question for me, "Do you want to know who you are?" There are times when God will ask people questions to foster a different way of thinking or to change the way they think so that they may know him for who he is in different seasons and stages of living life with purpose. *Worth the Struggle* is the sum total of every lesson learned during the journey or process of living your purpose. Needless to say, the task is best accomplished by knowing who God is first as his ordered steps guide people into their destiny.

Before Jerry's death, the most important role I had in his journey with ALS was transitioning from ex-wife to a type of Moses. As a type of Moses, my purpose was to get Jerry to the feet of Jesus. This is a place where I grew up as a child hearing God's word in hope that faith would fall into the root of things I faced that appeared to be a struggle in my mind. Sitting at the feet of Jesus was not a physical place that I went to, but it was a mindset I learned to develop in hope that all things would be possible by believing in who God is in his word. To get Jerry there, I had to overrule every reason why I divorced him, such as his ineffective coping skills and every uncertainty he had about how his journey with ALS would end. Because I believe that God is faithful, getting Jerry to the feet of God would be a place for him to find rest in his journey with ALS. Sitting at the feet of Jesus is a symbolic place where individuals are covered with his protection and are positioned for the overflow of who he is. Sitting at the feet of Jesus is the best seat in the house because it positions believers to trust that his word has power regardless of the amount received to change their life. God used Jerry's journey with ALS to demonstrate to me my role as a servant and the deep love he has for Jerry in spite of ALS. When Jerry needed to be cleaned or to have tears wiped from his eyes, to scratch his head, rub his back, brush his teeth, to be encouraged to eat, be escorted with assistance to and from the bathroom, I would imagine Jesus taking on this role as a servant but using me as a vessel to show his mercy and compassion. Weeks before Jerry's passing, I understood my purpose better. As a type of Moses, my purpose was to deliver Jerry to the feet of Jesus as the promised land. The ground I stood on and the purpose I played as a servant to Jerry in his journey were holy. God has the power and the control to create a holy assignment, place, or purpose from circumstances that are undesirable. "Then the LORD said to him, 'Take your sandals off your feet, for the place where you stand is holy ground'" (Acts 7:33). Before you were born, God had already prepared the ground in which you will stand as holy. This place is the place of purpose. God sees and is focused on purpose in spite of every negative thing people will say about you, including any and all undesirable lifestyle choices carried as extra baggage. God commands those things to be taken off that stand in the way or separate you from coming in the purpose he had already spoken into existence before you were born. This was the place where I had to look beyond Jerry being my ex-husband, the challenging physical work that was required from me and our sons in his daily care, and Jerry's reactions or the anger he had toward God for having to live with ALS. In my opinion, Jerry's attitude toward God because he had to live with ALS can be compared with Jesus's followers who found themselves having to deal with an unexpected storm and finding Jesus asleep in the boat. They had hoped to see Jesus fighting the effects of the storm beside them rather than sleeping peacefully. When his followers awakened him, Jesus quieted the wind and the water and questioned them about their limited knowledge of who he is as the author and finisher of their faith.

> Then His disciples came to Him and awoke Him, saying, "LORD, save us! We are perishing!" But He said to them, "Why are you fearful, O you of little faith?" Then He arose and rebuked the winds and the sea, and there was a great calm. So, the men marveled, saying, "Who can this be, that even the winds and the sea obey Him?"
>
> —Matt. 8:25–27

Faith is like a tool created to do extraordinary works. Believers are given this tool, but it works best when they understand the substance of faith. Jesus in the midst of a storm demonstrated to his followers that he is the substance of faith and the measure of faith they must work out of. The followers were concerned for the lives of everyone and the safety of the boat but didn't realize their source of faith is in knowing who Jesus is in the midst of any exasperating circumstance that pops up in this journey called life.

The substance of faith can be compared to deoxyribonucleic acid— the DNA of who Jesus is in connection to who God is. Our spiritual DNA is connected to who God is. Faith is the substance that empowers believers to relate to who God is in spirit and truth. God is looking for believers to develop into true worshippers by acknowledging who he is first while reaching and stretching toward being glad and rejoicing in the day that God has made. The state of being glad and rejoicing as true worshippers comes before the beginning of this is the day that the Lord has made. "Declaring the end from the beginning, and from ancient times the things that are not yet done" (Isaiah 46:10).

An effective illustration of an act of being glad and rejoicing in the day the Lord has made is Jesus's response after his followers asked him if he cared about their safety in the storm. Jesus responded with assurance that he is the substance of faith that brought peace on the boat and that quieted the storm. The substance of faith is knowing the core of who Jesus is. This knowledge can be obtained through cultivating a personal yet intimate relationship with Jesus. The name of Jesus is power all by itself, but what gives the name of Jesus power is the substance of who he is. Jesus is the substance that makes up faith and moves mountains out of the way for purpose.

> *Now God worked unusual miracles by the hands of Paul, so that even handkerchiefs or aprons were brought from his body to the sick, and the diseases left them and the evil spirits went out of them. Then some of the itinerant Jewish exorcists took it upon themselves to call the name of the Lord Jesus over those who had evil spirits, saying, "We exorcise you by the Jesus whom Paul preaches." Also, there were seven sons of Sceva, a Jewish chief priest, who did so. And the evil spirit answered and said, "Jesus I know, and Paul I know; but who are you?"*
>
> —Acts 19:11–15

Knowing the substance of who Jesus is becomes the core of a person's strength. This desire placed in the heart of a person to know Jesus empowers a believer. Being glad and rejoicing is the evidence of knowing who God is in spite of what appears to be problematic in the day the Lord has made. The believer uses the tools that God has given to become stronger in times of weakness and see an adversary as a distraction from being glad and rejoicing in the day the Lord has made. God will use such things as disabilities, lost wages, and dysfunctions in collaboration with his grace to make people stronger in their struggle and for his glory. Yet these same adversities can distract their thinking by having the adversities define who people are rather than what they are coming through. "The thief does not come except to steal, and to kill, and to destroy" (John 10:10). The evidence of worship is being glad and rejoicing in the day the Lord has made regardless of feeling uncertain about how the day will end. The adversary uses challenges as distractions to kill, steal, and destroy the acknowledgment of who God is through worship. The adversary knows that if the evidence of who God is can be taken away or destroyed, it will weaken a person's argument of who God is and discourage individuals from reaching the place of rejoicing and being glad in the day the Lord has made.

Every day the Lord has made instructs and encourages followers to have a transformed mindset in understanding who Jesus is in this is the day that the Lord has made. "For in him we live and move and have our being" (Acts 17:28). In Christ Jesus, we live out our purpose and finally become everything that God intended in our destiny. As followers move toward change in the process, their mindset becomes transformed into the mindset of Jesus. This process provides followers with the ability to rejoice and be glad in every circumstance. God's great faithfulness is a game changer! His faithfulness empowers believers to say, "Let us rejoice and be glad in it," before the day even gets started simply because the one who created the day is the one who commands believers to be glad and rejoice. Knowing and understanding the value of God's great faithfulness empowers believers that even if their faith comes up short, his faith is big enough, more than enough, and so far beyond measure that it can change the outcome of every game because he is true and faithful to his word. Moreover, God stands by followers in faith who love him—people who are called according to his purpose. God's faithfulness is not only a game changer, but it is the final say of any game, any circumstance, and any day. The challenge for some is not the measure of faith that has been given but believing in the one whose faith is so great and more than enough to make up any deficit or lack of faith from any believer. If only every follower could believe in God as the substance of who he is, the quantity of faith would never be questioned because God's faithfulness is more than enough. This concept leads followers to the point of rejoicing and being glad in the day the Lord has made.

Worship can plant seeds of truth in areas of our lives where depression, which is a form of inward anger, can later disturb our sense of peace. True worshippers can learn to use anger or depression as a source of energy toward worshipping God rather than as a source of self-destruction. The challenge for so many is understanding the substance of what faith is when feeling depressed, hopeless, and helpless. The parable of the wheat and tares in Matthew 13:28–30 is enlightening:

> He said to them, "An enemy has done this." The servants said to him, "Do you want us then to go and gather them up?" But he said, "No, lest while you gather up the tares you also uproot the wheat with them. Let both grow together until the harvest, and at the time of harvest I will say to the reapers, 'First gather together the tares and bind them in bundles to burn them, but gather the wheat into my barn.'"

Resting in the word of God through worship becomes an effective coping skill that empowers people in moments of surprise attacks from the adversary as they continue to work toward their purpose. At times in this is the day that the Lord has made, people will be at risk for depression when dealing with adversities. God is always in control over every circumstance that can appear as a barrier to discovering and fulfilling one's purpose. In the parable of the wheat and tares that Jesus shares with his followers, adversity also plays a purpose in our destiny. What God is illustrating as it relates to the kingdom of heaven is God's got this! Even the challenges that are necessary in this is the day that the Lord has made while discovering one's purpose; he has them too!

God is constantly waiting for believers to become empowered to overcome struggles with adversities through him regardless of whether the adversity appears to be as big as a giant in their eyes. Worship is a tool that can be used to fight against adversities such as depression, hopelessness, and helplessness. Likewise, the energy from feeling depressed and angry can be directed to worship and not used as weapons to harm oneself or others. This can happen when a person thinks like Jesus. "Be anxious for nothing, but in everything by prayer and supplication, with thanksgiving, let your requests be made known to God; and the peace of God, which surpasses all understanding, will guard your hearts and minds through Christ Jesus" (Philippians 4:6–7).

The Book of Job is one of many places in the Bible that can be used as an example to help others quickly understand that the struggle is worth it; although, there are times in the process that challenging steps are ordered by God for them to see his glory. "Though He slay me, yet will I trust Him" (Job 13:15). This type of mindset can also provide more insight into how God is faithful when a person encounters adversity in believing. "This is the day the Lord has made; let us rejoice and be glad in it."

Matthew 15:21–28 tells about a woman who initially was seeking healing for her daughter and learned that the help she really needed would require her to dig deeper into the substance of who Jesus is and not where he is positioned among others. This woman whose daughter was suffering from a demon-possessed spirit chose to leave her daughter at home as she went in pursuit of Jesus. It wasn't until she tapped into the substance of who Jesus is by revelation that she understood how concentrated and powerful Jesus is regardless of how others perceive who he is or his current position among others. Regardless of the amount of food she could get from the king's table, she knew that understanding who Jesus is as her source would be more than enough to change her and her daughter's life forever, seeing him as her only source of connection to her faith. "The eyes of your understanding being enlightened; that you may know what is the hope of His calling, what are the riches of the glory of His inheritance in the saints" (Ephesians 1:18). The woman with the issue of blood for 12 years chose to leave her sickbed in hopes of living an abundant life by becoming connected to the substance of who Jesus is. These two women learned that reaching toward the substance of who Jesus is was the source that empowered their faith through him, not the position people perceived him to be in. The transformation process is where the thinking of followers is changed into a mindset like that of Jesus.

> *(For the weapons of our warfare are not carnal, but mighty through God to the pulling down of strong holds;) Casting down imaginations, and every high thing that exalteth itself against the knowledge of God, and bringing into captivity every thought to the obedience of Christ.*
>
> —2 Cor. 10:4–5 KJV

God is so faithful to the substance of who Jesus is that all things are possible to believers. However, for believers, this concept begins from a transformation of the old way of thinking into a new way of thinking. The day the Lord has made is so much more than just another day filled with challenges. The day the Lord has made is a journey that incorporates the plans he has for people to succeed, where every ordered step leads toward destiny. The process often is mistaken as a trial of faith rather than as an opportunity to build faith in seeking who God is and the discovery of followers' true identity:

> *For the gifts and the calling of God are irrevocable. For as you were once disobedient to God, yet have now obtained mercy through their disobedience, even so these also have now been disobedient, that through the mercy shown you they also may obtain mercy. For God has committed them all to disobedience, that He might have mercy on all.*
>
> —Rom. 11:29–32

The gifts God has given are perfect, and his grace and mercy are wrapped around the gifts and callings he places in imperfect people.

Yin and yang are elements in a Chinese philosophy. According to the dictionary, "Yin is one of the two opposing principles whose interaction is believed to influence everything in the universe. Yin is negative, dark, and feminine, while yang is positive, bright, and masculine." The challenge is learning how to balance the yang and yin of the perfect gifts and callings that take up residence in an imperfect vessel of people created to serve God. People who master the balance of what appears to be imperfect and perfect in their eyes will be less judgmental toward the imperfections of others in their journey of discovering destiny. God's faithfulness is so great that it overpowers and rules out frustrations, fears, and doubts that others may experience time after time in this is the day that the Lord has made. God is faithful even when we are not, regardless of the step we are on and how effective or ineffective we are in coping on the step. The gifts of God will not be returned to him until they do what he purposes them to do. Situations or steps in this is the day that the Lord has made attract both yang and yin. Yang can be viewed as God's faithfulness and mercy and yin our doubts, fears, and frustrations. Yet God stands faithfully more in his word than in what people can ever do to cause him to regret any gift he has given, simply because he is omniscient. Because God is omniscient, he empowers and encourages others to believe in what he has spoken over their lives before the manifestation of their purpose. The depth of who God is stems from followers who believe in who he is as the Scripture states, their relationship with him, and the application of faith to their works. "You believe that there is one God. You do well. Even the demons believe—and tremble! But do you want to know, O foolish man, that faith without works is dead" (James 2:19–20)?

Some followers rejoice and are glad in the day that the Lord has made because they understand the steps throughout the day are preordered in the process of seeking him. The journey to discover who God is and to gain a better understanding of the substance of faith is governed by God's grace through the power of the Holy Spirit. On March 18, 2019, early Monday morning, Jerry went home to be with the Lord—to sit at his feet. Faith and God cannot be viewed by the human eye since he is spirit while faith is the substance of who God is. Only the Holy Spirit can reveal to people's minds and hearts who God is. "For we walk by faith, not by sight" (2 Corinthians 5:7).

> *Now faith is the substance of things hoped for, the evidence of things not seen. For by it the elders obtained a good testimony. By faith we understand that the worlds were framed by the word of God, so that the things which are seen were not made of things that are visible.*
>
> —Heb. 11:1–3

Since the day Jerry was made aware of his prognosis with ALS, I saw and heard his fears, doubts, and frustrations. This experience taught me in my own personal walk with God that frustration comes around to distract believers who are walking by faith and to discourage them from trusting him. The spiritual darkroom is a good example that fears, doubts, and frustration can be expected to show up. However, the presence of these emotions should not be looked upon as something wrong or a feeling that should be discouraged. Individuals facing adversity while going through a spiritual darkroom can easily become fearful, doubtful, and frustrated in their faith walk. Rather than judging people when they have these feelings, perhaps what they need to hear is a validation that it's OK and that these feelings are to be expected, but it is not God's intention for people to stay in them because he is faithful. The adversary is an opportunist and will use fears, doubts, and frustration against those who are faithful. The adversary will tempt them to believe that if God really loved them, he would not allow frustration to walk along with faith. It's through fear, doubtfulness, and frustrations that believers develop tenacity in their faith walk.

> *For an angel went down at a certain time into the pool and stirred up the water; then whoever stepped in first, after the stirring of the water, was made well of whatever disease he had. Now a certain man was there who had an infirmity thirty-eight*

years. When Jesus saw him lying there, and knew that he already had been in that condition a long time, He said to him, "Do you want to be made well?" The sick man answered Him, "Sir, I have no man to put me into the pool when the water is stirred up; but while I am coming, another steps down before me." Jesus said to him, "Rise, take up your bed and walk." And immediately the man was made well, took up his bed, and walked.

—John 5:4–9

Jesus, who is faith, was attracted to this man who was clearly frustrated with the process of becoming healed. He shared with Jesus every reason why he became so easily frustrated during the 38 years of trying to get healed without any success until he saw his struggles served a purpose. Likewise, Jerry was clearly fearful, doubtful, and frustrated with living with ALS and its disease process. However, I believe Jerry finally came to a point where he began accepting that the struggle had purpose, and he saw his destiny as being much greater than living with ALS and the dying process. Jesus was offering the man who had the infirmity for 38 years a different format in becoming healed.

In his last few days, Jerry stopped asking for healing from ALS but wanted rest from his discomfort. This is why I believe I had to get him to the feet of Jesus, where I knew he would find the rest and comfort he was looking for in the promises that God placed in his word. Jesus used me as a servant in providing rest and comfort by bringing our family to sit with Jerry in his last couple of days living with ALS. God arranged for me to cook comfort foods that weekend for our family, who gathered from different parts of Virginia and the Carolinas to celebrate Jerry's life and his accomplishments. God used me to open my home where Jerry found a sense of rest and comfort in coping with ALS. We saw God becoming faithful to us by outweighing the fears, doubts, and frustrations we faced living with a loved one who had ALS. As a type of Moses, I was able to bring Jerry to the feet of Jesus by providing what I had in my hand: homemade comfort food out of my kitchen and a home for Jerry and family members to rest in.

Learning to live with the challenges of living life with purpose is to know that it is worth going through the struggle. One of the lessons I learned was that the struggle was always intended to lead me back to the one who gave me purpose. At that time, I had thought that the process of learning to live life with purpose would have been much easier without any struggles in living out my purpose. However, the experience taught me to trust the God who attached the struggles to living life with purpose. I had to believe that it will work out for my good and his glory in spite of the struggle. Furthermore, it was a struggle for me to understand how the struggle can be attached to purpose and still work for his glory and for my good. The only thing that made sense was to give the struggle back to God and the plan he placed inside me for my purpose to work effectively and for his glory. Understanding that the struggle is worth it, individuals discover more and more about their purpose on a day-to-day basis, including the ordered steps and the lessons learned along the way of this personalized faith walk with God. Faith as it relates to purpose or destiny is a required tool in the process. Without faith, it is difficult to desire or please God. Faith will attract believers, but strangely enough, it also attracts fear, frustrations, unbelief, and doubts to hang around in people's thoughts even as God is attracting them to believe. Followers soon learn the art of balancing their faith in God's word as more powerful than their frustrations, fear, doubt, and unbelief as they come to know and believe that God is faithful to those who are struggling to believe.

> Now Thomas, called the Twin, one of the twelve, was not with them when Jesus came. The other disciples therefore said to him, "We have seen the Lord." So he said to them, "Unless I see in His hands the print of the nails, and put my finger into the print of the nails, and put my hand into His side, I will not believe."
>
> —John 20:24–25

"Jesus said to him, 'Thomas, because you have seen Me, you have believed. Blessed are those who have not seen and yet have believed'"

(John 20:29). Understanding the balance between faith, frustration, beliefs, and doubts is what gives rise to followers rejoicing and being glad to a form of worship. It's in knowing that God's plans for people are guaranteed to succeed regardless of what type of day they are having. Consequently, God's plan becomes more of a reality than what is happening to followers in the natural because believers have taken on this new thought process. Having this mindset of Jesus empowers people to see situations differently from what appears with the natural eye and their old way of thinking. Some people may have seen Jerry's illness and the dying process as frustrating and hopeless. But God allowed me to see an opportunity to bring Jerry to the feet of Jesus where he could find hope, rest, and comfort in the one who is faithful in our struggles.

> *Now to Him who is able to do exceedingly abundantly above all that we ask or think, according to the power that works in us, to Him be glory in the church by Christ Jesus to all generations, forever and ever. Amen.*
>
> —Eph. 3:20–21

God's promises makes the struggle worth it in the process for people to live life with purpose simply because . . . "this is the day that the Lord has made."

Lightning Source UK Ltd.
Milton Keynes UK
UKHW020650160920
370007UK00011B/575